CANADA

PATHWAYS TO THE PRESENT

JOHN SAYWELL

First published in 1994 by
Stoddart Publishing Co. Limited
34 Lesmill Road
Toronto, Canada
M3B 2T6
(416) 445-3333

Canadian Cataloguing in Publication Data

Saywell, John, 1929–
Canada : pathways to the present

ISBN 0-7737-5681-7

1. Canada – History. 2. Canada – Politics and government. 3. Canada – Economic policy. I. Title.

FC164.S38 1994 1994 C94-931319-X
F1026.S38 1994

Cover concept: Angel Guerra
Cover design: Brant Cowie/ArtPlus Limited
Printed in Canada

Canada: Pathways to the Present is a major revision and expansion of the author's earlier book, *Canada Past and Present*, which was published in 1982 by Clarke, Irwin, and has been translated into French, German, Italian, Spanish, Portuguese, and Japanese.

The author and publishers have made every effort to contact and credit the copyright owners of the photographs and illustrations reprinted in this book. The publishers would welcome information regarding any omissions or inaccuracies that may exist.

Stoddart Publishing gratefully acknowledges the support of the Canada Council, the Ontario Ministry of Culture, Tourism, and Recreation, Ontario Arts Council, and Ontario Publishing Centre in the development of writing and publishing in Canada.

Contents

PROLOGUE *1*

1 The Land and the People *4*

2 The Struggle for a Continent *17*

3 The Making of a Nation *26*

4 Building a National Economy, 1869–1945 *38*

5 Facing the Global Challenge *50*

6 The Lawmakers: Parliament and Politicians *60*

7 Ottawa and the Provinces *73*

8 The Conflict of Cultures *83*

9 The Road to a New Constitution—and Back *101*

10 The Charter of Rights and Freedoms *113*

11 The World Beyond *126*

12 Canada's Prime Ministers: Heroes or Villains? *142*

EPILOGUE: WHERE ARE WE? *158*

Prologue

ONCE DESCRIBED as the "Peaceable Kingdom," Canada today is under seige from without and racked by divisions within. Canada seems to have become a bewildered society, a nation blind to the new global realities that have seized it. A sense of community has been overwhelmed by an obsession with individual rights and the concerns of special interest groups. Divisions created by history and geography combined threaten to disrupt or even destroy the political institutions that were designed when the nation was founded. The economy, struggling under structural weakness and economic and political globalization, cannot endure the strain placed upon it. Life is no longer easily divided between what is private or public, economic or social, federal or provincial, national or international; all has become a seamless web. Politicians seem unable to lead and find nothing to follow.

Yet, as Canadians, we remain among the most fortunate people on earth. The problems we face—soaring deficits, unemployment, endangered social programs, ethnic tensions—are not unique to Canada, nor are they as severe as the problems of other nations. We continue to be among the wealthiest and healthiest countries in the West. Despite all our faults, we are a free and democratic people, and have been able to offer our land as refuge to the impoverished and oppressed throughout much of our history.

Most of us have voted with our feet in choosing to remain or become Canadians; we prefer to be here rather than there, even if we are not sure where here is. For Canadians have long been a people in search of a national identity, a quest that has proven as elusive as it is pointless. There is not for Canadians what Abraham Lincoln called that "mystic chord of memory" binding us together. Each Canadian eventually makes his or her own personal identification with the country, be it out of a passion for homegrown art or literature, or out of the immediate emotional surge one feels when an athlete such as Miriam Bédard wins an Olympic gold medal.

Our sense of being Canadian is filtered through the landscape that surrounds us, and the visual and emotional images evoked in each Canadian are as unique to the Prairie farmer as to the logger of the British Columbia rain forests. The Canadian identity is also filtered through our ethnic backgrounds and the years or generations we have spent in this new land. It is filtered through our sense of history, and the accomplishments of those who undertook the arduous task of building Canada. Being Canadian is not to subscribe to some overarching national mythology or dream, but rather, arises from a private sense of belonging.

It is now fashionable to write Canadian history in terms of injustice and repression, to raise the victims throughout history to heroic stature: native people, women, workers, immigrants, and other minority groups. More broadly, there is a trend that views the history of Canada as the ruthless exploitation of Eastern and Western Canada by the financial heartland, symbolized by Toronto and Montreal. And if these accounts of victimization are not complete, there are those who portray Canada as a country caught in the tentacles of a rapacious American economic and cultural empire. Denigration of the past is a necessary antidote to using history as cultural propaganda, but too often its purpose is less to understand the past than to ransack it for ammunition in some contemporary ideological debate.

It is, of course, almost criminal to compare Canada to other nations in the attempt to justify or diminish our shortcomings. Our captains of industry have not been more ruthless than those in other countries; and today our system of welfare, workers' compensation, and unemployment insurance is policed by a light hand that writes large cheques. French and then British and then Canadian governments have not been more ruthless in their treatment of the First Nations peoples than the American, Spanish, or Portuguese governments. Women were not more repressed in Canada than elsewhere, and got the vote and expanded their participation in the workforce at about the same time as in other western nations. Canada has not waged wars of aggression, and in tumultuous times has been an advocate and practitioner of peaceful diplomacy. We have probably been no more rapacious in our attack on nature than other countries; it's just that nature has been our major sustenance—and for many still is. Only recently has the realization dawned that our natural resources are dwindling and will have to be protected and preserved for continued use and enjoyment.

Canada is a product of its past, but Canadians need not be prisoners of that past. Canada is not a culmination of centuries of a common history, language, and culture; it is a new nation of disparate and diverse geographic and economic, cultural and linguistic communities. Ironically, it is only our history that explains us, and central to understanding this history is grasping how our institutions were created, and how the policies and practices that somehow give us that elusive sense of being Canadian were formulated.

The purpose of this book is to examine how we came to be, and therefore, who and where we are. Years ago I wrote a little book, *Canada Past and Present,* that attempted to explain Canada to people from other nations. It now seems an appropriate time to provide a new look at how Canada came to be, and to ponder whether Canada as we know it is likely to continue. For the divisions within the country—regional, cultural, and economic—have seldom run as deep as they do today.

1 The Land and the People

THE SHEER SIZE OF CANADA is overwhelming. It sprawls from the rolling crests of the Pacific to the crashing breakers of the Atlantic, from the northern Arctic ice fields, to the American border. With the breakup of the Soviet Union, it is now the largest nation on earth.

Canada is a land of infinite variety: of majestic stands of cedar and fir, and shady groves of maple and poplar; of the towering peaks of the Rockies, and the rounded, ancient granite of the Canadian Shield; of lush ranch land, and seemingly endless rolling prairie; of rivers that reach thousands of miles inland, and of possibly more lakes than exist in the rest of the world combined; of quiet sandy beaches and coasts where the mountains plunge into the sea. Canada contains millions of miles of untamed and untapped wilderness—only seven percent of which can be cultivated. And yet there are parts of the land that have not escaped the plough for 400 years.

It is a land of small elevator towns, logging camps and mining settlements, of fishing outports, and trappers' shacks. It is a land of cities: the breathtaking beauty of Vancouver; the soaring skyscrapers of commercial Toronto; the French flair of Montreal; the old fortress of Quebec overlooking the St. Lawrence; the port of Halifax, whose ancient guns still frown menacingly over the harbour. It is difficult to fathom Canada's vastness and variety.

The enormity of the country has, in fact, continually been a threat to its existence. Most of its 28,000,000 people are stretched out in a ribbon along the length of the southern boundary. The vapour trail of a 747, the gleaming tracks of two transcontinental railways, and the tarred thread of the Trans-Canada Highway link Canada's Atlantic and Pacific coasts. Travelers can only marvel that the nation exists, for crossing the country they see not one Canada but many. Geography does not divide Canada from the United States nearly so much as it divides sections of the country from one another.

The four Atlantic provinces, home to only one Canadian in five, are the northern-most extension of the Appalachian Mountains, which run along most of the Atlantic seaboard of North America. For 500 years, fishermen from Europe have harvested the waters off the East Coast, the first fishing settlements in Newfoundland beginning almost 400 years ago. From the weathered homes in the tiny outports of Newfoundland and the towns along the Nova Scotian coast, fishermen have tested their skill and courage against the cold and angry Atlantic waters. Their harvest has always yielded a poor living, and today, with the stocks of fish depleted because of overfishing, the future looks bleak. But offshore there is hope for new riches, as gigantic oil rigs probe beneath the icy waters in search of oil and gas.

Farmers still till the rich soil of Prince Edward Island, as they have since the French Acadians settled there almost 300 years ago. Only a few hundred remained after the British conquered New France, but they were soon replaced by immigrants from the British Isles. Farming is still by far the most important industry for the 125,000 Islanders, but the coast is also rich in lobster and other shellfish. And of course, thanks to the legendary Anne of Green Gables, tourists flock to the Island to see the famous heroine's home.

New Brunswick forests once supplied masts for the British navy that ruled the North Atlantic, but today the timber meets its fate at sawmills and pulp and paper plants. Small subsistence farms have almost disappeared from New Brunswick, but large farms produce twenty percent of the potatoes in Canada, and companies there, such as McCain's, process large quantities of food for export.

Clearing the land in New Brunswick, 1834. New Brunswick is the only Atlantic province where the significant French population (thirty percent) reflects the early history of the Maritimes. The three mainland Atlantic provinces were first called Arcadia, and later, Acadia, by the early explorers. Initially settled by the French, Acadia was taken by the British during the prolonged French-English wars of the eighteenth century. In 1755 the British started to expel the Acadians, but some returned after the peace of 1763, and in 1800 there were about 3,800 Acadians in New Brunswick. (Today there are over 25,000.) The first major British settlements in New Brunswick were established by 14,000 Loyalist refugees who fled the American colonies during the Revolution. But they were outnumbered by waves of immigrants from the British Isles in the early nineteenth century, who came to work in the booming lumber industry and clear the land for settlement in the river valleys.

New Brunswick Museum.

The Atlantic provinces have been little affected by modern immigration. Most of the inhabitants are descendants of people from the British Isles, some families having lived in the region for generations or even centuries. The people of the Atlantic provinces may be poorer than the average Canadian, but they have a strong sense of independence, a distinctive outlook rooted in their past, and a sense of identity as "Maritimers"—those who live by the sea.

United by geography but divided by language and culture, the provinces of Quebec and Ontario form two distinctive

Canadian regions and societies. For almost 400 years Quebec farmers have cultivated narrow strips of land running back from the St. Lawrence. Logs flow down turbulent rivers from the Canadian Shield to feed the hungry mills. From out of the Shield, too, railways bring minerals yielded grudgingly from the ancient mass of volcanic and granite rock. The raging rivers of the Shield have been harnessed to provide hydroelectric power that feeds the industries of Quebec, Ontario, and New York, and in the past twenty years a vast territory around James Bay has been inundated and rivers diverted in perhaps the largest hydroelectric project in history. As compensation for the use and partial destruction of their land, the Cree and Inuit were paid $225 million and were given exclusive hunting and fishing rights and a large degree of self-government.

Eighty percent of the people in Quebec are French-speaking. While most now live in the larger cities, whose industries produce almost one third of Canada's manufactured goods, the quiet farms and villages and the white towers of the parish churches constantly reveal what the province was like for several centuries, and for some still is.

Across the border in Ontario, the most populous province, the floor of the St. Lawrence Valley broadens. The farms become larger, and the settlements run many miles north of the river. Prosperous farmers, dairy producers, and fruit growers in the Niagara Peninsula generate one third of the nation's agricultural wealth. In the bleak wilderness of the Shield in Northern Ontario, a string of towns and cities live off the rich yield of the forests and mines. But the pulse of the province comes from the large manufacturing cities that sweep around Lake Ontario from Niagara Falls through Toronto and on to Oshawa. This "golden horseshoe" is the largest manufacturing region in Canada and Toronto is its capital.

The southwestern portion of the Canadian Shield gradually disappears into the wheatlands of the Canadian Prairies, one of the great granaries of the world. The Prairie provinces—

Once second to Montreal, Toronto is now the nation's undisputed financial and business capital, with Canada's largest stock exchange, and the head offices of most of the major banks, insurance companies, and Canadian and foreign corporations. It is also the centre of the English-language media and communications empires.

Toronto Stock Exchange.

Manitoba, Saskatchewan, and Alberta—were largely settled in the early years of this century. This region is populated in part by the descendants of British, French, and American settlers, but the descendants of the myriad of Central European peoples, who came to build the railways and open the land for settlement, now make up half of the Prairie population. Today the Prairie provinces are no longer completely dependent on farming and ranching. Oil in Alberta and to a lesser extent in other provinces, potash and uranium in Saskatchewan, and gold and nickel in Manitoba have broadened the economy of the region and provided greater prosperity.

Beyond the Rockies lies British Columbia, a province extremely rich in natural resources—mainly forests, water, and mines. Much of British Columbia's abundant hydroelectric power is exported to the United States, and the province boasts of a rapidly growing manufacturing industry based on raw materials. While the capital city, Victoria, retains a quiet old-world charm, much of the province's activity is on the mainland, on the edge of the frontier, where life is vigorous and dynamic. Many British Columbians tend to regard their beautiful province as an empire in itself. And increasingly it is an empire, one that looks across the Pacific to market its natural resources and to find the capital to finance its economic development. For British Columbia, Canada is a Pacific nation and Vancouver its economic capital.

Stretching across the top of the four western provinces are the giant Northwest Territories and the Yukon. Governed partly from Ottawa, but hoping eventually to become provinces, the North makes up forty percent of Canada's area. Yet in that vast Arctic region there are only 82,400 people. Many of them are Inuit and Indian, although increasing numbers of newcomers now live in the North as prospectors, engineers, oil explorers, merchants, government officials, and operators of the radar lines and air bases that guard the northern links to the continent.

Native peoples in the North and in the rest of Canada are making the transition from their traditional lives of hunting and fishing to participate in the modern economic life of the country. They are also rewriting history. Acknowledged as "First Nations" people, native groups are attempting to reclaim some of the land that was once theirs, seeking compensation for past injustices, and demanding a large measure of self-government in order to preserve their unique culture and identity.

The aboriginal peoples were the first Canadians. But they, like all Canadians, were once immigrants to a new land. Most anthropologists now agree that these first Canadians crossed over from Siberia during the last Ice Age, when there was a land bridge over what is now the Bering Sea. From the North they spread south and east to the Atlantic coast and the southern tip of South America. When the Europeans arrived there were about half a million Amerindians in what is now Canada.

Over the next 300 years contact with the Europeans decimated the aboriginal population, bringing not only a radical transformation in their traditional ways of life, but also diseases for which they had no natural resistance. In the census of 1881 there were only 100,000 Indians in Canada, and by 1930 some scholars believed they would disappear completely.

Ancestors of the Plains Indians had been hunting on the plains for 10,000 years before the Europeans arrived. Spanish colonists in Mexico had brought the horse to the continent, and through trading and warfare the horse gradually spread north and reached the Canadian plains in about 1730. There were then about 33,000 Indians on the Prairies divided among the Blackfoot, Gros Ventre, Cree, Ojibwa, Assiniboine, Stoney, and Sioux.

Life on the plains revolved around the buffalo. As one fur trader observed: "The wild ox supplies them with everything which they are accustomed to want. The hide of this animal, when dressed, furnishes soft clothing for the women; and dressed with the hair on it, clothes for the men. The flesh feeds them; the sinews afford them bow-strings. . . . The amazing number of these animals prevents all fear of want. . . ."

Glenbow Museum.

But improved medicine and nutrition and a very high birthrate led to a rapid increase in the native population, and today there are 500,000 aboriginal peoples registered as Indians and perhaps another 500,000 who either are not registered or have mixed European and Indian ancestry, a people known as the Métis.

About seventy percent of registered Indians live on lands "reserved" for them, while the rest have moved to cities in search of jobs. The nonregistered Indians are scattered across the country, although the largest group of Métis live in the

Prairie provinces, where their ancestors intermarried during the days of the fur trade.

There also over 30,000 Inuit who live in the Canadian Arctic. Although there were earlier inhabitants, the ancestors of the present-day Inuit arrived in Canada from Alaska about 1,000 years ago, and lived a semi-nomadic life fishing, hunting, and gathering food, largely undisturbed by European settlers. But since World War II the economic development of the North has brought the Inuit much closer to the mainstream of Canadian life.

The first Europeans to settle in Canada were the French. The 6,500,000 French Canadians living in what is now Quebec are the offspring of the 60,000 people who lived there when the British conquered New France in 1759. Quebec is still the heartland of French Canada, but many French-speaking people live in New Brunswick and Ontario, and others are scattered across the country.

Less than half the population of Canada trace their origins to the British Isles—England, Scotland, and Ireland—and of these many are the offspring of marriages between British and other immigrants. The British came after the conquest from Britain and the United States. Migration continued throughout the nineteenth century, and by 1900 almost sixty percent of the population was British and thirty percent French. But the ethnic mix of Canada began to change in the decade and a half before World War I, when three million "new" Canadians arrived to settle the Canadian West and to work in the rapidly expanding factories, mills, and mines. Although one in three was British, the majority of immigrants were from Central and Eastern Europe. More came in the 1920s, but the Great Depression and World War II effectively stopped immigration between 1930 and 1945. Then, in the twenty years after the war, another 2.5 million people fled war-torn Europe to seek a better and more peaceful life in Canada.

As late as 1961, however, ninety-seven percent of Canadians were of European origin. Canada had not yet welcomed

Emigrants by the ship *Ganges* departing for Canada. Although over 1,500,000 immigrants entered Canada during the last thirty years of the nineteenth century, more people left Canada for the more prosperous farms and factories of the United States than entered. In fact, many of the immigrants were bound for the United States, but found it easier to enter through Canada.

Royal Ontario Museum.

immigrants from non-European countries; the only significant non-Europeans were the 50,000 Asians in British Columbia. Indeed, as late as 1947, Prime Minister Mackenzie King stated that Canada did not "wish as a result of mass immigration to make a fundamental alteration in the character of the Canadian population." But in the 1960s the racial barriers began to come down. Not only was the European influx dwindling, but racial discrimination became less acceptable to Canadians. When Canada's immigration policy became "colour-blind," the pattern quickly changed, and by the mid-1970s there were more immigrants from Asia and other Third World countries than from Europe. By the 1980s over seventy percent of new arrivals were coming from Asia, Africa, and Latin America. This pattern remained in the 1990s.

These newest of the new Canadians have radically and permanently altered the human landscape of the country. Today one Canadian in fifteen belongs to a "visible minority." Moreover, most immigrants move to large urban centres upon arrival; Toronto alone is home to one out of three, and almost four out of ten residents of Toronto and Vancouver are foreign-born. By the early 1990s, thirty percent of Vancouverites are of Asian origin.

Canada has become a truly multicultural society. In 1971 Pierre Trudeau's government officially endorsed the policy of multiculturalism, and established a government department with a large budget to promote the multicultural character of the country. Some scoffed that it was only a cynical attempt to catch the ethnic vote. Others believed it was an appropriate response to the diverse and changing nature of Canadian society, but waited to see if government promotion of multiculturalism would become something more than "folk dancing and feathers." Nevertheless, multiculturalism was embedded in the 1982 Charter of Rights and Freedoms, which instructed the courts to interpret it "in a manner consistent with the preservation and enhancement of the multicultural heritage of Canadians . . ."

Canadians have always thought themselves a tolerant people and many have considered their country a "cultural mosaic," where cultural differences were valued. But, in truth, unless earlier immigrants were prepared to stay out of the mainstream of Canadian life, by and large they were expected to assimilate to the language, behaviour, and cultural norms of the host society, and until they or their children did so they would be subject to discrimination. The growing visibility of nonwhite immigrants tested Canadian values and revealed that intolerance and discrimination can exist here, too. In the early 1980s the federal government responded to the growing evidence of racial discrimination by establishing a Race Relations Directorate within the Ministry of Multiculturalism. And in 1988 the Mulroney government's Canadian Multicultural Act provided that the government should assist "ethno-cultural minority communities" in conducting activities with the hope of overcoming any discriminatory barriers and, in particular, discrimination based on race or ethnic origin.

There was an inevitable, if small, anti-immigration backlash in Canada, due in part to a high rate of unemployment. This was most clearly seen in the increased opposition to a very relaxed policy towards refugees. Canada had long been a haven for many refugees: from Russian tanks in Hungary and Czechoslovakia; from the horrors of Idi Amin in Uganda; for 100,000 Vietnamese "boat people" in the 1980s; and from the brutality of the civil war in Somalia in the 1990s. However, throughout the 1980s thousands of immigrants somehow arrived in Canada and boldly and falsely claimed they were refugees. When two boatloads of such people walked ashore in Nova Scotia, there was a national outcry that forced the government to tighten refugee admission procedures.

By the early 1990s Canadians were obviously ambivalent about the impact of the latest wave of immigration on Canadian society. A public opinion survey in the spring of 1994 revealed that while seventy-three percent believed that "a mixture of different lifestyles and cultures makes Canada a more attractive place to live," at the same time most Canadians believed there were "too many immigrants," especially those of visible minority groups (*Globe and Mail*, 11 March 1994). Six out of ten agreed that "too many immigrants feel no obligation to adapt to Canadian values and way of life." And a survey in December 1993 indicated that seventy-two percent believed that "the long-standing image of Canada as a nation of communities, each ethnic and racial group preserving its own identity with the help of government policy, must give way to the U.S. style of cultural absorption" (*Globe and Mail*, 14 December 1993).

C'EST VOTRE BIBLIOTHÈQUE
AYTH EINAI H BIBΛIOΘHKH ΣAΣ
這是你們的圖書館
ਇਹ ਤੁਹਾਡੀ ਲਾਇਬ੍ਰੇਰੀ ਹੈ
यह आपका पुस्तकालय है
یہ آپ کی اپنی لائبریری ہے
QUESTA È LA VOSTRA BIBLIOTECA
ESTA ES SU BIBLIOTECA
ISTO É A SUA BIBLIOTECA
DIES IST IHRE BÜCHEREI
EZ AZ ÖN KÖNYVTÁRA
TO JEST WASZA BIBLIOTEKA
ЦЕ ВАША БІБЛІОТЕКА

"This is your library."

The debate over immigration and multiculturalism and the growing evidence of racism is clearly on the current political agenda. But it is dangerous for those on either side of the debate to overreact. The influx of visible minority Canadians is changing the face of many of our urban neighbourhoods without undermining the structure of Canadian society. The process of mutual accommodation and interaction is slow. It is also often painful, particularly for parents who are watching their children become Canadians, retreating from or discarding their home culture as they go to school, get jobs, fall in love, and marry. Prem Kumar, an immigrant from India, put it this way:

> *To thousands of Indo-Canadian children, now attending junior or senior high schools in Canada, India is a distant and foreign land. Neither language nor religion binds them to her. India's staple foods—lentils, rice, chapatti, chutney—don't excite their palates. A very large number of these youngsters have anglicized their names. Bob, Don, Dave, Ken, Sheila, Karen, Dolly are names not just confined to mainstream*

> *Canadians. In their ignorance, some white Canadians call Indian youngsters "East Indians" or "Pakis." The truth is these youngsters are out and out Canadians, imbued with the attitudes and manners of any typical Canadian youth. ("Scenes from an Indian Marriage,"* Policy Options, *March 1994)*

The real challenge may be to worry less about immigrants and multiculturalism and more about the negative attitudes and sometimes racist behaviour of many mainstream Canadians with whom that younger generation of immigrants is assimilating. The federal government's poster campaign in 1994 proclaiming "Racism. It's up to you" was an attempt to change those attitudes. But the government, too, must realize that dramatic increases in immigration make the process of adjustment and accommodation on all sides more difficult. Tolerance and accommodation are essential, however, for the course has been set and the human face of Canada has been altered forever.

2 The Struggle for a Continent

LIKE OTHER COUNTRIES IN THE AMERICAS, Canada is an offshoot of Western Europe. The East Coast of North America was discovered by Europeans—Spaniards in the South, and English, French, and Dutch in the North—all seeking a westward route to Asia. The cry of "LAND! LAND!" from Columbus's weary and frightened sailors in 1492 was echoed and re-echoed from the mainmasts of the ships of Cabot, Corte-Real, Verrazano, Cartier, Gilbert, Raleigh, and Hudson until most of the coastline was discovered and mapped. The early attempts of both England and France to start colonies failed, and the sixteenth century ended with only the Spanish and then the Portuguese firmly established in the Americas.

But Europeans were still drawn by the mystery of America, and by the search for a passageway to China through a continent that, to a vast extent, remained unknown. At almost the same time the French and English both established permanent colonies in North America. In 1607 the Virginia Company founded Jamestown, and soon hundreds and then thousands left England to settle in the New World, either to improve their fortunes or to escape religious persecution. By the end of the seventeenth century much of the coastline had been settled, and by the middle of the eighteenth century about 1,500,000 people lived in the thirteen colonies in what is now the United States.

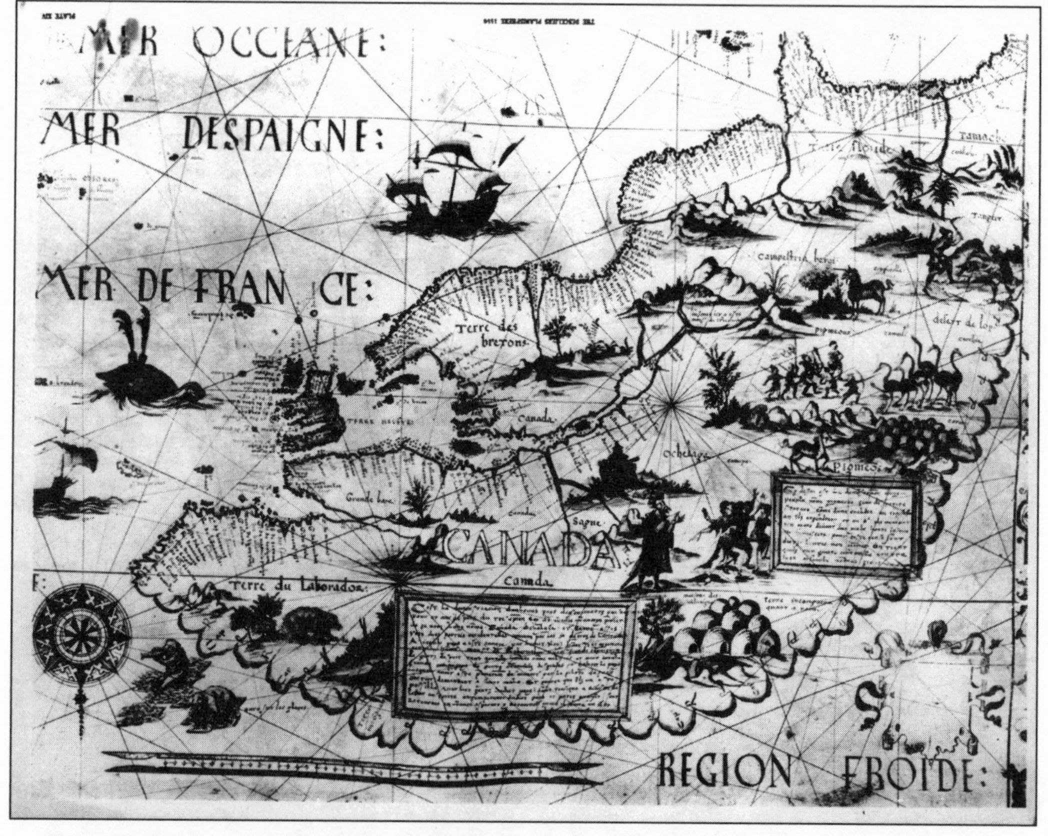

This map represents the state of knowledge about Canada soon after the initial voyages by Jacques Cartier to the St. Lawrence between 1534 and 1542. National Archives of Canada.

Explorers, fur traders, and adventurous settlers were already looking beyond the Appalachian Mountains towards the rich lands of the Ohio–Mississippi Valley. Once the mysteries of the mountain passes had been solved and the interior discovered, the stage was set for a war that would determine the future of Canada, for the colony of New France stood in the way of the English.

The story of New France, or Quebec, had a different course and a different ending from that of the thirteen American colonies. Ordered to find gold and a passage to Asia, Jacques Cartier had first discovered the entrance to the St. Lawrence River, which he called Rivière du Canada, in his second expedition in 1535, and sailed up to what is now Montreal. But the French soon lost interest in exploring the New World, and it was only in 1608 that Samuel de Champlain established the first French foothold on the cliff overlooking the St. Lawrence at Quebec City.

Yet those few people had carved out a far-flung empire for France in North America. In the St. Lawrence–Great Lakes waterway the French had a communications system, which, once mastered, opened up the entire interior of the continent from the Gulf of Mexico to the Rocky Mountains. Adventurous fur traders, the *coureurs de bois,* and explorers pressed along the water routes, followed and sometimes preceded by courageous missionaries determined to convert the Indians.

Champlain was one of the great explorers of North America. He established an alliance with the Indians along the St. Lawrence and Ottawa rivers, and with the Hurons around the southern Great Lakes. He explored and mapped the Upper St. Lawrence, the Ottawa River, Huronia, and the lake in New York State that bears his name. But settlers did not flock to his new colony and when he died in 1635 there were only 100 or so people in Quebec. There was never to be a mass migration to New France, as the French seemed less willing to leave Europe than the British. Moreover, the climate in New France was harsh, much of the land unsuitable for agriculture, and for many decades the small colony was under attack by the Iroquois. By the 1760s there were only 60,000 settlers in New France.

Nova Francia Accurata Delineato 1657. This map, drawn by a French priest, reveals the state of knowledge about Ontario and the Iroquois country to the south. The insert shows Huronia, the site of perhaps the most celebrated missionary activities. Ste. Marie among the Hurons, built by the missionaries, was destroyed in 1650 when the Iroquois destroyed the Huron Confederacy, but has been reconstructed on its original site near Midland, Ontario.

National Archives of Canada.

In 1642 the city of Montreal was started at the head of navigation on the St. Lawrence, beyond which oceangoing ships could not sail, and became the centre of the canoe-based fur trade. Before long, French fur traders had reached west to Lake Superior and north to Hudson Bay. Every year saw the French push farther into the depths of a continent unknown to Europeans, usually with the assistance of the Indians, with whom they traded. In 1672, Louis Jolliet, a priest turned fur trader and explorer, was ordered to find the Mississippi River, described by the Indians as the "great father of waters," to see whether it flowed west to the Pacific or south to the Gulf of Mexico. Setting out from Montreal, Jolliet and Father Marquette reached Michilimackinac, where Lake Michigan flows into Lake Huron. The following spring they paddled by way of Lake Michigan and finally reached the Mississippi. They followed it hundreds of miles south until they knew it was not the route to the Pacific. Nine years later the Cavelier de La Salle went down the river to the Gulf of Mexico, claiming the land for King Louis XIV of France, and naming it Louisiana.

Other explorers and traders moved westward. The greatest was Pierre Gaultier de Varennes de la Vérendrye and his two sons, Louis-Joseph and Jean-Baptiste. Promising to find the fabled river to the Pacific, Vérendrye was given a monopoly of the fur trade west of Lake Superior. Between 1730 and 1740 they built a string of fur-trading forts from Thunder Bay to Lake Winnipeg and beyond to the Saskatchewan River. Indians told them of another river to the south that led west. In 1742 they explored the Missouri River, and the Mandan Indians told them of great mountains farther west. They turned their faces westward, and on New Year's Day, 1743, saw the Black Hills of the Dakotas. There is some evidence that in 1748 Louis-Joseph and his party were the first to see the towering peaks of the Rockies.

By this time the stage was set for a war that would determine whether the British or the French would control the destiny of Canada and much of North America. The immediate flash point was the string of French forts that lined the

Ohio–Mississippi Valley and prevented American expansion westward. But in many ways the struggle between the French and the English was as old as the first settlements themselves. The French and English had fought over Hudson Bay, where the British had established a fur-trading company in 1670. They had fought over the French colony of Acadia, now Nova Scotia, and it was passed back and forth several times before France ceded it to the British in 1713. But the French then built the fortress of Louisbourg on Cape Breton Island to guard approaches to the St. Lawrence. For years the Richelieu River–Lake Champlain region and the upper Hudson and Mohawk valleys were aflame with skirmishes. The Iroquois, allies of the British, had repeatedly attacked the tiny French colony strung out along the St. Lawrence. The French and their Indian allies attacked British settlements near the border.

The final struggle between English and French for the continent really began in 1754 when a young militia colonel, George Washington, led a small force to expel the French from the Ohio Valley and to clear the way for British traders and settlers. The so-called French and Indian War in North America soon became part of the worldwide struggle for trade and empire between France and England. From America to India the British fleet and British arms were eventually triumphant.

With the British capture of Louisbourg in 1758, and Quebec in 1759, French power in North America was shattered. In the

---

Illustration, right: Quebec, 1759. The British army under General James Wolfe tried to capture Quebec from Montmorency, but the attack was a bloody failure. For weeks Wolfe hesitated, but was finally persuaded to try a surprise attack above the city. As his men moved up the river in small boats at night, a French sentry cried out, *"Que vive?"* A quick-thinking Highlander whispered in perfect French, *"La France."* The unsuspecting sentries were overpowered, and by dawn the army was drawn up on the Plains of Abraham. Rather than stay inside the city, the French commander, Montcalm, chose to fight on open ground. Both generals were killed, but Wolfe lived long enough to know that victory was his.

National Archives of Canada.

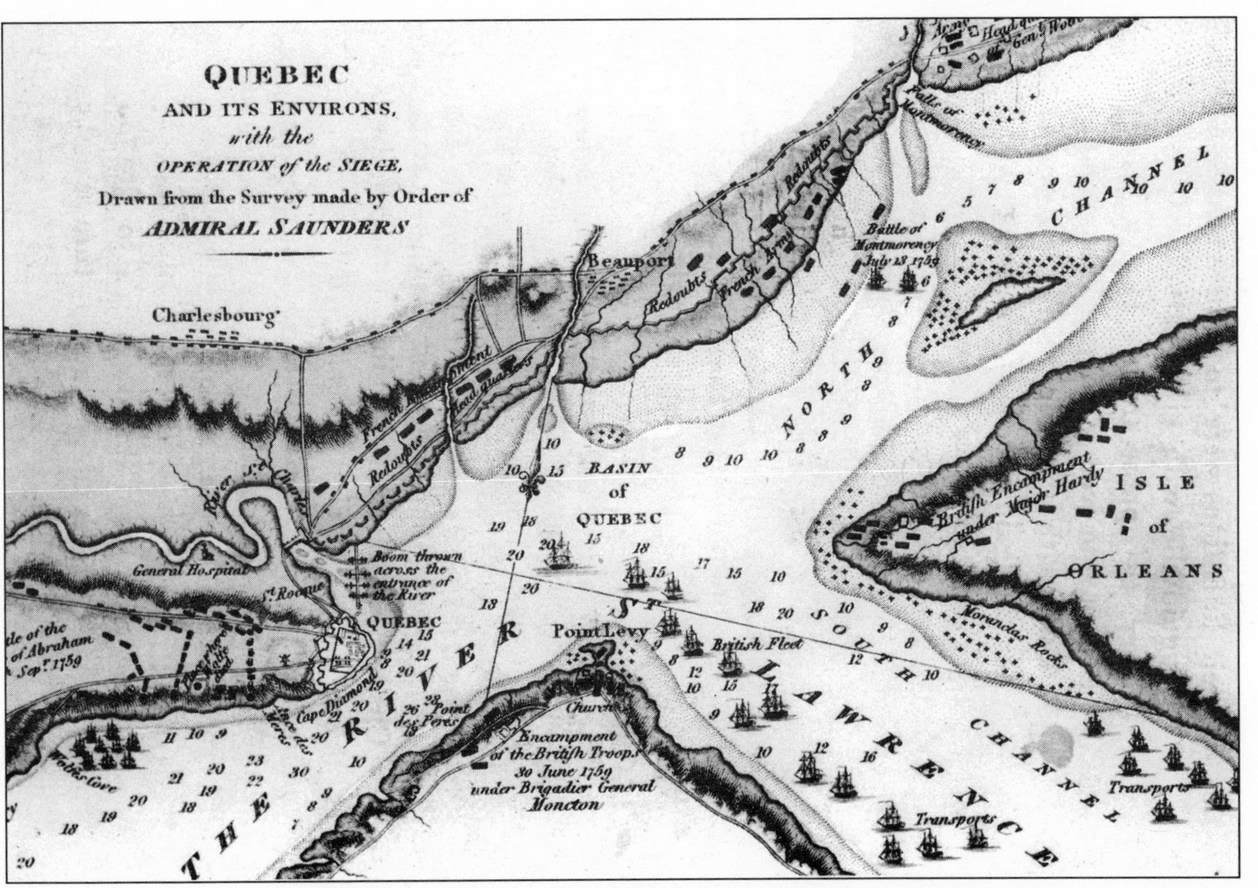
QUEBEC
AND ITS ENVIRONS,
with the
OPERATION of the SIEGE,
Drawn from the Survey made by Order of
ADMIRAL SAUNDERS
Charlesbourg
Beauport
Redoubts
French Army
Falls of Montmorency
Battle of Montmorency July 18 1759
NORTH CHANNEL
BASIN of QUEBEC
Boom thrown across the entrance of the River
General Hospital
St. Roque
QUEBEC
Cape Diamond
Point des Peres
Point Levy
Church
Encampment of the British Troops 30 June 1759 under Brigadier General Moncton
British Fleet
Transports
ISLE of ORLEANS
British Encampment under Major Hardy
Morandas Rocks
SOUTH CHANNEL
THE RIVER St. LAWRENCE
Wolfes Cove
of Abraham Sept. 1759

peace treaty of 1763 New France became another British colony in North America. The struggle for the continent seemed over. Yet twenty years later North America was to be divided once again, when thirteen of the British colonies successfully won their independence from Britain.

Strangely enough, the conquest of New France was itself a major cause of the American Revolution. To pay for the recent war against France and to meet the expense of controlling the Indians in the newly conquered western territories, the British government decided to secure some of the needed revenue in the North American colonies. The new taxes enraged the Americans and led to the cry of "no taxation without representation," and finally to revolution. Moreover, the removal of the French threat ended the old reliance on British troops to defend the colonies and made the Americans more willing to assert their independence.

British policy towards the recently acquired western territory also fanned the embers of revolution. In the Quebec Act of 1774 Britain announced that the Ohio–Mississippi Valley would be closed to settlement and would remain as it had been before the conquest of New France—a fur-trading area governed from Quebec. The Americans were furious. The conquest of New France had been in vain; once again they were prevented from expanding westward. The guarantees in the Quebec Act that the French Canadians could use their own language and remain Roman Catholics further outraged the largely Protestant Americans. The Quebec Act was regarded as one of the "intolerable acts" that led to the American Revolution.

When the first Continental Congress met in Philadelphia in the fall of 1774, the second phase in the struggle for the continent had begun. One of the first acts of the Congress was to invite Quebec and Nova Scotia, the two northern colonies, to send representatives. They were "the only link wanting to complete the bright and strong chain of Union," read the invitation, and, "a moment's reflection should convince you which will be most for your interest and happiness, to have all the rest of North America your unalterable friends, or your inveterate enemies. . . . Be assured that the happiness of a people inevitably depends on their liberty."

The appeal fell on deaf or suspicious ears. In Quebec the Roman Catholic clergy had no love for the Protestant Bostonians nor for the radical cry for liberty and democracy. The French-Canadian peasants were largely indifferent. The British officials and troops were hostile. In Nova Scotia the people were unlikely to listen to the appeal since they lived their lives under the shadow of the British fortress at Halifax and depended, for much of their livelihood, on that great naval base and the profitable trade with Britain. When it was clear that American agents could stir no revolutionary spirit among the inhabitants of the fourteenth and fifteenth colonies, General George Washington decided to capture Quebec before the British could send reinforcements. Two armies moved north into Canada in 1775. One captured Montreal and joined the second outside the walls of Quebec City. But they were unable to capture the city, and when a British fleet appeared in the spring of 1776 the tattered remnants of the liberation army fled.

While Quebec and Nova Scotia remained aloof, the thirteen original British colonies, supported by France and Spain, engaged in a fierce struggle for their independence. What they could not readily achieve by force of arms they were able to accomplish by skillful diplomacy. Britain was soon quite anxious to see the end of the revolutionary war. As a result, American diplomats were able to secure a very favourable peace treaty. In 1783 Britain agreed to recognize the independence of the thirteen colonies. And while she rejected the American request for all of British North America, Britain gave the United States all of the Ohio–Mississippi country.

At one stroke of a diplomat's pen the historic connection of the St. Lawrence and the Ohio–Mississippi Valley had been ignored and the future of the continent shaped. North of the Spanish territory, continental North America was divided between an independent, English-speaking United States, and two British colonies, one of which was overwhelmingly French-speaking. In a geographical sense the American Revolution fathered not only the United States, but Canada, too.

3 The Making of a Nation

The American Revolution helped shape the physical framework of modern Canada by drawing the southern boundaries of the new British colony of Quebec and cutting it off from the Ohio–Mississippi Valley. It also helped to define the Canadian population. During the Revolutionary War and its aftermath, over 40,000 Americans who had remained loyal to Great Britain moved north to settle in the remaining British colonies; 35,000 of these United Empire Loyalists, as they were called, moved to Nova Scotia, many of them settling on the virgin lands of what became New Brunswick. Another 7,000 moved overland to the shores of the St. Lawrence and Lakes Erie and Ontario.

Here was the nucleus of a new British colony in the heartland of the continent. Behind the 7,000 came the so-called Late Loyalists, Americans who, in order to get free land, claimed they had been loyal to Britain. Behind them came thousands of ordinary American pioneers, ignoring political boundaries in the search for new land. In 1791 this new area was separated from the old French colony of Quebec and was given the name Upper Canada (now Ontario); Quebec was renamed Lower Canada. By 1812 Upper Canada had 80,000 people, four out of five of whom had come from the United States.

The existence of such a large American population in Upper Canada worried the British Governor when the United States declared war on Britain and her North American

When war was declared in 1812, Isaac Brock, British commander in Upper Canada, quickly captured Detroit, then moved back to Niagara where he expected the main American attack. In October the Americans lauched a surprise attack on Queenston. Racing seven miles up the river from his headquarters, Brock gathered a handful of men and some Indian allies and charged the Heights. Although he was killed, the invasion was arrested, and a thousand American soldiers surrendered. Upper Canada was safe for the moment.

National Archives of Canada.

---

colonies in 1812. The war was largely the result of tensions on the high seas, for as Britain fought a life and death struggle against Napoleon she frequently played havoc with American shipping. But it was also the result of continuing rivalry and tension in North America. The United States still looked enviously on the Great Lakes area, while many British North Americans still hoped to undo the Revolution and regain control of the Ohio–Mississippi territory.

The conquest of Canada was not "a mere matter of marching," as one American anticipated. Indeed, the Americans did better in single-ship engagements with the British navy on the Atlantic than against the small force of British regulars and Canadian militia that defended the frontier. In 1814, with Napoleon defeated in Europe and Britain able to send large numbers of tested veterans to North America, Britain and the United States made peace. The war had ended in a stalemate; the peace treaty restored the status quo.

Within the next few years Britain and the United States agreed to demilitarize the Great Lakes and to extend the Canadian–American boundary along the forty-ninth parallel to the Rockies. As a result, the end of war began a policy of reasonably peaceful coexistence and further confirmed the division of the continent along its present lines.

The British North American colonies grew quickly after the Napoleonic Wars ended in 1815. By 1850 more than 500,000 immigrants had arrived, and the population leaped from under 500,000 in 1815 to over two million. The settlers came largely from the British Isles—from the armies that had fought Napoleon, from the bleak factory towns of the new industrial England, from the Scottish farms that barely sustained life, and from Ireland where emigration was often the only alternative to starvation.

Some of the newcomers settled in Nova Scotia to work in the lumber camps, the shipyards, or the fisheries, or to join the fleets engaged in trade with New England and the West Indies. Thousands of families went to New Brunswick, whose lumber was in great demand in the shipyards and the growing factory towns of England. The largest number went to Upper Canada, where they quickly carved farms out of the bush that pressed down upon the lakes and rivers, or became tradesmen, merchants, or teachers in the increasing number of pioneer towns.

All the colonies were strongly tied to Britain, for there was the market for timber, grain and flour, potash, and furs. Under the system of imperial preference, the British let colonial goods into the Mother country almost duty free, giving them a marked advantage over goods from other countries, who had to pay a tariff duty, making their goods more expen-

Most of British North America was heavily dependent on the timber trade. Trees were cut and trimmed and pulled to the river before spring. When the ice broke, they were squared, bound together in rafts, and floated down the rivers to waiting sawmills or to ports whose ships carried the timber to England.

sive. However, since goods from the United States passing through Canada could also enter Britain free of duty, Americans shipped their grain to Canada where it was milled and exported to England. Canada thus built up a flourishing commercial life, based not only on its own farms and forests but also on transporting and processing American products. Despite the political boundary, the St. Lawrence waterway still functioned as the route to the interior of the continent.

But by 1849 the colonies' commercial system had collapsed. During the 1840s the United States had forbidden Americans to trade via the St. Lawrence, and was enticing Canadian products to move to Europe through American ice-free ports. The real blow was delivered by the British, however, when in 1849 they adopted free trade. No longer would the colonies enjoy special treatment in Britain; their goods would have to compete on equal terms with those from Europe and the United States. The Canadian merchants were distressed. In Montreal, the commercial and financial centre of Canada, some businessmen signed a petition urging annexation to the United States.

Yet the situation was not as bleak as it looked. World trade improved in the 1850s and Canadian goods were in demand in Britain and Europe. The booming American farms and cities, where population doubled between 1840 and 1860, provided growing markets for Canadian lumber and foodstuffs. In 1854 a reciprocity treaty with the United States provided for free trade across the border in the principal natural products, and greatly increased North–South trade. Finally, the railway boom brought increased work and prosperity, and really sparked the early industrialization of Canada. In 1850 there were only sixty-six miles of track in Canada, compared to 6,000 miles in the United States. But during the 1850s the Grand Trunk was built west from Montreal along the St. Lawrence to Lake Huron, and east to the winter port at Portland, Maine. The Great Western linked Detroit and the Niagara River, and short lines ran north from Lake Ontario to tap the farms and forests. By 1867 there were over 2,000 miles of track in British North America.

Although the boom collapsed in 1857, prosperity returned with the outbreak of the American Civil War. Yet the Civil War also threatened the long-term prosperity and even the survival of British North America. Canadians were opposed to slavery—both the Canadas and Nova Scotia had for years been a haven for runaway slaves—and thousands of Canadian men joined the Union army. Nevertheless, the colonists had mixed feelings about the war. Might not a victorious North with its great expansive energy and its sense of "Manifest Destiny" turn its huge army northward?

This possibility was made more likely because of British policy during the Civil War. British opinion was divided, with probably a majority favouring the North. Yet the British government permitted Southern raiders, like the *Alabama*, to be built in British shipyards. In 1862 Britain almost went to war when a Northern warship, the *San Jacinto*, stopped the *Trent*, a British mail ship, and removed two Southern diplomats on their way to England. So serious was the danger of war that Britain immediately sent heavy reinforcements to Canada.

To many Northerners, Canada itself did not seem to be impartial. There was considerable anti-Canadian feeling, for example, when in October 1864 Confederate agents raided St. Albans, Vermont, from Canadian soil. The raiders were captured by the Canadians, but when they were released there was an outburst of anti-Canadian feeling in the North.

Even before the Civil War there had been signs that the reciprocity treaty might not be renewed because of the opposition of Americans who had to compete with Canadian products. The tension of the Civil War made the end of reciprocity a certainty, and forced Canadians to search for another solution to their economic problems. Why not follow the American model, many Canadians asked, and try to find strength through a national union? Why not create a nation that would include the Maritime fisheries, the farmlands and factories of the Canadas, and the rich but untapped resources of the Prairies and British Columbia? Would not such a transcontinental economy offer a substitute within a new country for the old trade with Britain and the United States?

Speed in the pursuit of union was essential because there was the very real danger that the Prairie West and the Pacific Coast would fall into the hands of the United States either by peaceful occupation or force of arms. Although owned by Britain, the land from the Great Lakes to the Pacific was in the hands of the Hudson's Bay Company, which had only a string of fur-trading posts across the land. Between the Great Lakes and the Rockies the only settlement was on the Red River, near present-day Winnipeg, which consisted of 6,000

Métis, the offspring of French fur traders and Indian mothers, 4,000 descendants of English-speaking traders and Indian mothers, and 1,500 settlers and traders from Britain, Canada, and the United States. Red River's link with the outside world was through the American state of Minnesota, to the south. By the 1860s the frontier of American settlement had passed Minnesota. Farmers enviously eyed the vacant plains to the north, and American railway interests hoped to draw the western British territory into their orbit. At Red River itself a Washington agent was secretly working for its annexation to the United States.

The Canadians remembered what had happened in the Oregon territory, which also had been under the control of the Hudson's Bay Company. American settlers had organized in the 1830s and then demanded that the land become theirs. When the American government supported their demands and threatened war, the Company withdrew to Vancouver Island, and in 1846 the British gave what is now Washington and Oregon to the United States. Could not the same pattern be repeated not only on the Prairies but also in the colony of British Columbia? After all, thousands of Americans had flooded north when gold was discovered on the Fraser River in 1858.

There was even fear of an American invasion of all or part of British North America. Charles Sumner, chairman of the powerful Senate Foreign Relations Committee, was an outspoken advocate of the annexation of British North America. There were many Americans who supported him, partly in a desire to hurt Britain and partly because they believed it was the "Manifest Destiny" of the United States to rule the entire continent. The motley American army of 1812 had been stopped, but when the Civil War ended could battle-tested Union veterans be similarly repelled if they decided to march northward?

The main impetus for the union of the British North American colonies came from the Canadas. A union of Upper and Lower Canada (Ontario and Quebec), in 1840, had failed,

With the discovery of gold in 1857 on the Fraser River, thousands of miners moved north from California and around the world. The rush moved north up the river and onto the Caribou. Instant towns sprang up along the rivers and creeks and months later could be ghost towns. One such town was Emery's Bar, pictured here. By the late 1860s the rush was over and the colony faced an uncertain future. The American purchase of Alaska from Russia in 1867 suggested one fate that might await it.

Archives of British Columbia.

as cultural differences between the French and the English, along with their mutual competition for government favours, had paralysed the government of the colony. Both the Canadas wanted what they called "self-government," that is, the freedom to look after their own affairs. One obvious solution was to separate, but that would have led to economic and military weakness. Another was to create a federal union, where each colony would look after matters involving their own culture and institutions, but would agree to a central or federal government to handle the matters they had in common, such as the economy, transportation, and defence. However, at the same time, the Atlantic provinces were considering some form of union to solve their problems. Why not, then, a federal union of all the British colonies? The Canadians proposed the idea at a meeting with delegates from the Atlantic provinces at Charlottetown, Prince Edward Island, in 1864. The proposal was accepted and the details were hammered out during a conference at Quebec later in the year.

At Quebec, the delegates agreed that each colony would become a province, and each province would retain its own government. Provinces would elect members of a national House of Commons in proportion to their population. The Senate, or upper house, would be composed of members appointed equally from the three regions—the Maritimes, Quebec, and Ontario. The power to pass laws was divided by subject matter between the national and provincial governments, as we shall discuss in chapter seven. The British government, anxious to see a stronger and more independent British North America, supported the proposal with enthusiasm, and played an important role in encouraging New Brunswick, and forcing Nova Scotia, to join. In 1867, British Parliament passed the British North America Act, which brought the new nation into existence. But Prince Edward Island remained out until 1873, and Newfoundland only joined in 1949.

Before 1867 the two Canadas had been so jealous of each other that they had not been able to agree on a capital city. The government had moved back and forth between Quebec City and Toronto, when finally, in 1857, the Canadians asked the British to pick a capital. On the advice of the Colonial Office, Queen Victoria selected Ottawa, a lumber city situated on the river boundary between Quebec and Ontario. The first Parliament buildings had been completed in 1866, and Ottawa became the capital of the nation one year later. Sir John A. Macdonald, not the inventor of the federal union but the diplomat whose skills brought it to fruition, became the first prime minister of Canada.

One of the first tasks of the new Canadian government was to secure the West, as American expansionists were becoming more menacing. The Hudson's Bay Company was willing to sell the land, and the British were anxious that Canada take

With a population of 50,000 in 1867, Toronto was smaller than Montreal. The great age of railway building in the 1850s linked Toronto to Montreal, New York, Detroit, Chicago, and the Great Lakes system at Georgian Bay.

Metropolitan Toronto Reference Library.

it over. In the biggest real estate deal in Canadian history, Canada purchased the land west to the Rockies on up to the Arctic for $1,500,000, although the Hudson's Bay Company retained huge amounts of fertile land as well as the land around its posts.

Unfortunately, neither the British nor the Canadians had thought of the inhabitants of the Red River, the Métis. Fearful of the effect of white settlement on their way of life, the Métis contested the Canadian takeover. Led by Louis Riel, they seized Fort Garry, where Winnipeg now stands, and formed their own government. Riel then demanded that Ottawa agree to the creation of a province with its own government, the protection of the French language and Roman Catholic religion, and Métis ownership of their land.

In Ottawa, Macdonald reluctantly agreed to negotiate. In 1870 Red River became the tiny province of Manitoba, and the rest of the Northwest Territories were governed from Ottawa until 1905, when Saskatchewan and Alberta became provinces. Louis Riel was Manitoba's "Father of Confederation."

"The Situation" in the West as a contemporary saw it in 1869.

However, fearful of retaliation for the execution of an Ontario settler during the resistance, he fled before the Canadian Army arrived to assure the takeover.

The last step was the acquisition of British Columbia, with its population of 10,000 settlers and 25,000 Indians. Most of the Americans had left after the gold rush, but British Columbia had much closer ties with the United States than with Canada, and there was a very real danger of annexation. The United States had purchased Alaska in 1867, and the Americans in British Columbia appealed to their president to complete the occupation of the Pacific Coast. However, although the British government had no desire to keep the colony, it did want to have an all-red door on the Pacific and instructed the governor of the colony to support the Canadians who wished to join Canada. When the Canadian government offered to build a railway to the coast, take over the colony's debt, and provide financial support, the pro-Canada party won and the legislature unanimously voted to enter Confederation. On July 20, 1871, Canada reached the Pacific.

4 Building a National Economy, 1869–1945

EXPANSION TO THE PACIFIC had been the first major task of the new government elected in 1867 and led by Sir John A. Macdonald. For the next twenty-five years the Old Chieftain, as he became known, guided the destiny of Canada, attempting to bridge the differences of race, religion, and region to make the new nation a political and economic reality.

Sir John knew that unless blood and muscle could be added to the skeleton, the forces drawing Canada into the American orbit would become too strong to resist. What Canada needed was a "National Policy" of economic expansion and integration. As it took shape, the policy was composed of three parts: a transcontinental railway, a high tariff against foreign manufactured goods, and the settlement of the West. The tariff wall, which went up in 1879, would provide a protected market for Canadian manufacturers and would force foreign companies, who wished to sell in the Canadian market, to build factories in Canada. Settlers in the West, who could buy 160 acres of land for ten dollars, would produce wheat for export and increase the market for Canadian-made goods. The main artery of the land was to be the railway, carrying the lifeblood of the nation east and west along its twisting line of steel.

By the early 1880s the Canadian Pacific Railway was pushing across the plains, and a trickle of settlers—over 20,000 by 1885—had followed into the territories. But the West was not

The "Last Spike" to complete the Canadian Pacific Railway was driven at Craigellachie, B.C., on November 7, 1885. Built with the assistance of $25 million and 25 million acres of land from the government, the CPR was completed in four years. As in the United States, the railway recruited thousands of Chinese labourers to work on the western section.

The Americans had a much easier time building their first transcontinental, which was completed in 1869, for they did not have to fight the Canadian Shield around Lake Superior, and the western mountain ranges were much less formidable than in Canada.

Canadian Pacific Railway.

---

to be settled peacefully. Before the West could be opened for settlement, the government had to negotiate with the 25,000 Cree, Ojibwa, and Assiniboine Indians who inhabited the land.

In the woodlands, the Indians lived by hunting, fishing, and trapping. On the plains their lives revolved around the buffalo, which provided not only pemmican, the dried meat that was the staple in the diet of both the Indian and fur trader, but also clothing and shelter. But by the 1860s the giant herds of buffalo had almost disappeared and the future looked bleak for Plains Indians. With the West about to change forever, the Indian leaders had to choose between negotiating a treaty with the Canadians or fighting them, as many tribes were doing in the United States. Reluctantly, they chose to negotiate, and by the end of the 1870s had signed treaties in which they surrendered their land in return for their own reservations, schools, annual cash payments, and the provision of tools and equipment.

By the early 1880s, however, the Indians were restless and angry. They could not adjust quickly to life on the reservation and looked fondly back to the days when they had roamed the plains in search of buffalo. By 1883 Indian agents were reporting that the Indians were starving and needed more help from the government. The worried chief of the Northwest Mounted Police, which had been created in 1873 to maintain law and order in the West, bluntly warned the government that unless more aid was given to the Indians, "there is only one other solution and that is to fight them." But in Ottawa, Macdonald and his colleagues, who had not always lived up to their promises to the Indians, delayed taking any action.

The Métis in the Northwest were also restless. In an attempt to preserve their way of life, thousands of Métis had left Red River after 1870 to settle along the banks of the Saskatchewan River, where a small Métis community already existed. But the crops had been poor and there was little other work. Above all the government had refused to survey the land and guarantee them ownership of their new farms. Their appeals to Ottawa, like those of the Indians, went unanswered until it was too late.

The Métis turned once again to Louis Riel, then living in Montana. Riel returned to Canada, and in the spring of 1885 both the Métis and the Indians took up arms. The Northwest was aflame. Within days an army from Eastern Canada was on its way over the still unfinished railway and then faced an

Macdonald's promise to investigate the Indian and Métis grievances came too late for Riel and many Indian chiefs.

Grip, April 11, 1885.

---

overland march of several hundred miles to reach the Métis settlement at Batoche. Exhausted and without ammunition, the outnumbered Métis refused to surrender. But the end was inevitable. The Métis returned to their ruined villages and the Indians laid down their arms. The revolt in the West was over. But the hanging of Louis Riel for treason caused a conflict between French and English where peace, as we shall see, was more elusive.

Elsewhere in Canada there were also rumblings of discontent. Modern economists have shown that there was substantial economic growth in Canada in the 1880s, but that fact seemed less apparent to Canadians at the time. The National Policy did not seem to be bringing the expected prosperity; in fact, more people left Canada for the United States than arrived. In the election of 1891, the Liberals attempted to persuade the voters that reciprocity, or freer trade, with the United States was the only answer. The Old Chieftain warned that free trade would simply be the first step leading to annexation, bringing an end to the British connection and any hope for a Canadian nation. His emotional appeal to Canadians to vote for "The Old Flag, The Old Policy, The Old Leader" was successful. However, exhausted by the campaign, Sir John A. died a few months later.

The 1890s were lean years for Canada, but by the end of the decade Sir Wilfrid Laurier, who had been elected Liberal prime minister in 1896, could exclaim that "The twentieth century will belong to Canada." In the 1890s the worldwide recession was coming to an end and there was a revival of economic activity everywhere. The discovery of gold in South Africa and the Yukon increased capital for investment. Rapid industrialization in the United States and Europe increased the demand for and price of wheat and lumber, and improved shipping brought the costs of transportation down. Just as Canadian wheat became competitive on world markets, the free land that had attracted millions of immigrants to the United States was exhausted. The frontier of Prairie settlement turned north to the virgin lands of the Canadian West, where new cultivation techniques had solved the problems of lack of rainfall and early frosts.

Opening up the West, 1910.

Vancouver Public Archives.

Before 1914, more than one million people moved to the Canadian West from Eastern Canada, Britain, Europe, and the United States—including Canadians returning home from the United States. In 1905 the federal government created the provinces of Saskatchewan and Alberta, leaving only the Far North to be governed from Ottawa. The farms and the booming towns and cities provided an enormous market for lumber, equipment, and personal goods. And two new transcontinental railways thrusting from Eastern Canada to the Pacific needed thousands of workers, miles of rails, and engines and freight cars from eastern factories.

Although the emergence of the western wheat economy was the most spectacular development of the boom years, wheat was not the only engine of growth. The same years saw the discovery of silver and gold in Ontario; the exploitation of the rich mineral resources of British Columbia; the explosion of the forest industry, particularly pulp and paper; the harnessing of rivers for the production of electricity; and the dramatic growth in manufacturing—which increased six times between 1900 and 1914—particularly in Central Canada. Massive amounts of foreign investment from Britain and the United States financed the economic development. Many of the new industries either were financed by American capital or were the branches of American companies that wished to secure tariff-free access to the growing Canadian market. Canadians welcomed American investment until after World War II, when many became concerned that the country had become a "branch plant economy."

Yet, despite its apparent success, there were many who argued that the National Policy worked to their disadvantage. Western farmers complained that they had to sell on an open international market while paying the high cost of tariff-protected manufactured goods. Eastern farmers wanted better access to the American market. Many of the new industries—particularly pulp and paper and mining—had sprung up to serve the American market, and they, too, wanted easier access, as did their American owners or customers.

In 1911 the two countries signed a reciprocity agreement for freer trade in natural products and lower duties on many American manufactured goods. It seemed like a good deal for Canada, but the opposition was intense. All those interests involved in the East–West economy created by the National Policy—railways, banks, manufacturers, merchants—organized to oppose reciprocity when Laurier called an election in 1911. Wisely, they did not underline their economic interests, but launched a campaign to persuade the voters that reciprocity would sever the British connection and lead to annexation—an argument strengthened by boasts from American politicians that the Stars and Stripes would soon fly over Canada. Laurier and reciprocity were defeated.

The face of Canada had changed dramatically between Confederation in 1867 and 1914. The population had tripled to reach almost nine million. At Confederation seventy-five percent of Canadians were rural; by 1914 almost fifty percent were urban. Agriculture remained the largest single industry, but manufacturing was a close second as Canada was becoming an industrial society. Equally important was the emergence of what is called the "service sector"—the office, the

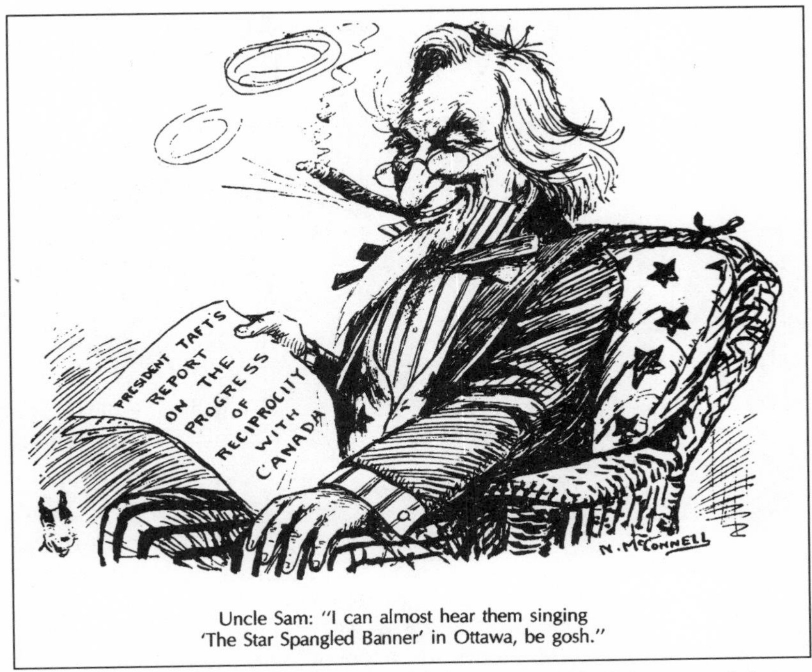

Uncle Sam: "I can almost hear them singing 'The Star Spangled Banner' in Ottawa, be gosh."

Months before the Reciprocity agreement was signed, the nature of the opposition was clear.

Toronto News, October 7, 1910.

---

bank, the store, with their armies of secretaries, managers, and clerks, and arsenals of typewriters, phones, and adding machines. These armies were increasingly composed of women—at least in the ranks.

World War I accelerated the economic development of Canada within the framework already built. Canadian farms fed the soldiers in France. Manufacturing almost doubled, as Canadian factories expanded to produce the goods previously imported from Britain, or were retooled to produce the instruments of war. With 600,000 men in the Army, women entered the industrial and agricultural workforce to replace them.

The end of the war brought a painful period of adjustment. Unemployment, high prices, and low wages led to a new

The appeal to the farmers to reject the old parties in this wartime cartoon was also successful. In the election of 1921 the farmers of Western Canada and Ontario, with some labour support, sent sixty-four members to the House of Commons in Ottawa.

National Archives of Canada.

militancy among workers, and there was a wave of strikes across Canada—the Winnipeg General Strike in 1919 the most violent among them. The farmers, still smarting over the defeat of reciprocity in 1911, saw prices decline dramatically, and in the West the crops were poor from 1918 to 1921. The farmers moved into politics, and by 1921, sometimes in cooperation with labour, formed United Farmer governments in Alberta, Manitoba, and Ontario, and sent sixty-four members of the Progressive party to Ottawa in the 1921 election. The political landscape had been changed forever as parties representing class and regional protests broke the dominance of the Liberal and Conservative two-party system.

The protests became muted as expansion and better times returned during the 1920s. The most dramatic growth came in resource development and manufacturing. Canadian natural resources—particularly pulp and paper and metals—were in heavy demand in the United States, and American capital financed much of the expansion. Manufacturing was fueled by two new technologies: the mass-produced automobile and the household use of electricity. Before the war the automobile had been a luxury of the wealthy; but by the 1920s the car was within the price range of the average Canadian. The arrival of electricity in the home created an enormous demand for stoves, refrigerators, and radios. By the end of the decade manufacturing was far more important than agriculture, and Canada had become a truly urban society. The service sector, too, was expanding rapidly, and consequently, more women were entering the workforce.

Looking back, it is clear that the 1920s witnessed the end of the "National Policy" period of Canadian history. The West had been settled, indeed oversettled, as farmers had filled up lands where the lack of rainfall made farming risky. The railways had been built, indeed overbuilt, as two transcontinental lines went bankrupt during World War I and had to be taken over by the government to become the Canadian National. The tariff had done its work, for better or for worse, and the pressure from many parts of Canada was to bring tariff walls down and lower prices for the consumer. It remained to be seen whether the federal government would find a new role for itself. But the Great Depression of the 1930s helped to answer that question.

The "Roaring Twenties" ended with a resounding crash when the world economy collapsed in 1929. As the United States and other countries erected protective tariff barriers, the markets for Canadian exports almost disappeared, and for some exports, like wheat, for which there was a market, the prices fell below the cost of production. To make matters worse, much of the Canadian West was hit by a severe drought, which for years made planting almost pointless. The decline in the export industries hurt every sector of the economy.

The 1930s produced many "crackpots" who believed they had the magic solution to end the Depression. One was William Aberhart, a high school math teacher and fundamentalist preacher, who founded the Social Credit party and led it to victory in Alberta in 1935. Aberhart believed the solution lay in increasing the amount of money people had to spend, and he issued "prosperity certificates," which he asked Albertans to use instead of money. The problem was that no one would accept these prosperity certificates and so the experiment with "funny money" failed.

Before the worst was over, one quarter of the population was unemployed and living off government relief. The politicians lacked the skill, the will, or the money to get people back to work, and Ottawa and the provinces spent much of the time arguing about who was responsible for the unemployed. Many cities and some provinces that had gone badly into debt in the 1920s to build the cities and their sewers, schools, hospitals, and the network of highways could not pay their debts and went bankrupt. Canada, like other nations, did begin to emerge from the Great Depression late in the decade, but it was really only Adolf Hitler and the onslaught of World War II, in 1939, that brought the world out of one tragedy and into another.

The Depression had a lasting effect on Canada. It not only revealed how fragile the economy was, but showed how vulnerable the individual and the family were in an industrial and urban society. Moreover, the inability of the federal and provincial governments to deal with the nation's problems suggested that there should be basic changes in the way the Canadian federal system, created in 1867, would work in the future. For the moment, however, such issues had to be set to one side as Canadians put all their efforts into stemming the Nazi tide.

World War II completed the transformation of Canada into a major industrial power. With Europe overrun in 1940, Canada stood behind Britain as the major Allied power. Even when the United States entered the war, Canadian factories and farms played a crucial role in the Allied war effort. In an unbelievably short time the Canadian economy was reconstructed to produce aircraft, ships, and armoured vehicles, and the production from farms, forests, and mines expanded enormously. Before the war ended almost a million men and women were engaged in war production, and another million men and women served in the Armed Forces. It was an impressive commitment from a nation of eleven million people. Canada had come of age.

5 Facing the Global Challenge

FOR TWENTY-FIVE YEARS AFTER THE WAR, although there were some ups and downs, the Canadian economy enjoyed a spectacular boom. After fifteen years of depression and war, Canadians had an enormous demand for homes, cars, and appliances, including the newest gadget on the market—the TV set. And the rebuilding of a devastated Western Europe provided markets for Canadian exports.

Most spectacular were the discovery and exploitation of new resources in Canada. The huge fields of oil and gas found in Alberta in 1947—and later in Saskatchewan and British Columbia—set in motion the laying of a massive network of pipelines to the markets of Eastern Canada and the United States. A year later one of the largest iron ore bodies in the world was discovered in Northern Quebec. The construction of the St. Lawrence Seaway by Canada and the United States in the 1950s made it possible to move the ore to the steel mills, and allowed oceangoing ships to steam 2,000 miles inland to the head of the Great Lakes. New fields of uranium, the source of nuclear energy, were found in Saskatchewan and Ontario, and Canada became a world leader in the powerful uses of nuclear power and the export of uranium. Potash, the key element in fertilizers, was discovered in Saskatchewan in the 1950s, and Canada soon supplied forty percent of the world's trade.

There was an insatiable demand for power to fuel the economic expansion in Canada and the United States. Many Canadian rivers close to urban centres had already been tapped, but with new engineering and transportation technologies, larger and more distant sources could be harnessed. Over the years engineers tapped the enormous energy in the Columbia and Peace rivers in British Columbia, the Nelson in Manitoba, the Ottawa in Ontario, the Manicougan–Outard rivers in Quebec, and Churchill Falls in Labrador. Production of hydroelectricity increased five times between the end of World War II and the mid-1970s, and continued to grow with the completion of the first phase of the massive James Bay project in Quebec in the 1980s.

The postwar economic boom drew Canada increasingly into a closer relationship with the United States. Canada remained, as it always had been, highly dependent on foreign trade. Among the leading postwar exports were pulp and newsprint, lumber, wheat and other agricultural products, crude oil, and minerals. Canadians also imported more manufactured goods per person than any other country on earth, and this pattern of exporting natural resources and importing manufactured goods was disturbing. Also disturbing was the increasing level of trade with the United States, which, by the 1970s, accounted for seventy percent of both Canadian exports and imports. Less than ten percent of foreign trade was with Britain and Europe. Japan had become Canada's second largest trading partner, but with only five percent of our overall trade Japanese trade did little to diminish our dependence on the United States.

The same was true of capital investment. Like all young countries, Canada had relied heavily on foreign capital. Until 1914 much of this capital came from Britain, but after the war our economic expansion had been financed by the Americans. By the 1970s they were responsible for seventy-eight percent of all foreign investment. Americans owned or controlled more than half of Canadian manufacturing, mining, smelting, and the oil and gas industry. In some fields—aluminum, rubber, and automobiles—American ownership was almost 100 percent. One indication of the increasing

The Monster that Ate America

Concern about the level of American ownership of the western oil and gas industry prompted the Trudeau government to introduce the National Energy Program in 1980. The NEP increased the federal share of the profits at the expense of the oil companies and the provincial governments, and provided that only *Canadian* companies could explore for oil in lands owned by the federal government in the North. The Act outraged the American government, the companies, and the provinces, and President Ronald Reagan and members of the American Congress denounced it as an attack on free enterprise. Under pressure from the Americans some of the provisions were watered down by Trudeau. But it was not until Brian Mulroney became Prime Minister in 1984 that the entire program was killed. Cartoonist Roy Peterson mocks the American outrage.

---

integration of the two North American economies was the 1965 Auto Pact, which guaranteed a fair share of the North American market to firms based in Canada.

By the 1960s and 1970s many Canadians—particularly on the political left—were concerned that this heavy reliance on the United States threatened Canadian independence. The government did respond with attempts to diversify Canadian trade, control American investment, and increase Canadian participation in the oil and gas industry, much to the annoyance of American and Canadian business. But the pattern of increasing dependence—or interdependence, as some called it, because the Americans relied on Canadian raw materials—continued.

Taking everything into account, Canada was producing over five times as many goods and services by the mid-1970s as it had been at the end of World War II. The population had doubled, and among the manufacturing and trading nations of the noncommunist world Canada ranked seventh in its Gross Domestic Product (GDP), the measure of economic strength. However, the six other nations—the United States, United Kingdom, Germany, France, Italy, and Japan—have from two to ten times the population, and in terms of per capita GDP, Canada ranked third.* Furthermore, in the 1970s, Canadians enjoyed one of the highest standards of living in the world.

They also enjoyed the benefits of what has been described, with some exaggeration, as "cradle to grave" social security. The Depression had revealed that in a modern industrial society the individual is often helpless when faced with unemployment, and even in good times many are unable to pay high medical bills or save enough for their old age. But there was an obstacle to the development of a social security system in Canada: under the Constitution of 1867, responsibility for social security lay with the provinces, and even during the Depression the courts had denied the federal government the power to enact unemployment insurance legislation.

However, during and after World War II, the federal and provincial governments found ways to implement a national

*Those are the Group of Seven (G7) nations whose prime ministers meet annually at an economic summit to attempt to find common approaches to the economic problems of the world.

security system. In 1940 the provinces agreed to an amendment to the Constitution to give the federal government authority over unemployment insurance, and by the 1970s payments to the unemployed were among the most generous anywhere. Between 1957 and 1968 Ottawa and the provinces agreed to introduce hospital insurance and medicare; Ottawa set national standards and paid half the costs, but the provinces ran the programs. Ottawa also agreed in 1966 to pay half the costs of provincial social assistance, or welfare, programs. And in 1965 all the provinces except Quebec agreed to a national old age pension plan; Quebec established its own, but it was almost identical to the national plan. There were pessimists at the time who argued that the country could not afford such expensive programs. But in the boom years of the 1960s everything seemed possible.

The optimism was short-lived. In the early 1970s the "global economy" was convulsed by sudden and severe increases in oil prices, which led to inflation and a worldwide slowdown of economic activity. As a nation with twenty-five percent of its economy based on international trade, Canada could not be immune to the economic decline. Economic growth slowed down; wage and price controls were necessary to control inflation; and during the worst years of the so-called Great Recession of the early 1980s, an unemployment rate of eleven percent was the highest since the Great Depression. Although conditions improved a little in the mid-1980s, the world barely recovered when it went into another recession late in the 1980s, from which it was still recovering in 1994.

With tax revenues declining as a result of the economic slowdown while the costs of dealing with the unemployed were rising, governments went increasingly into debt. By the mid-1980s the Canadian deficit, the difference between government revenues and expenditures, was a major political issue. Each year the deficit added billions to the national debt, on which heavy interest payments threatened to consume over twenty-five percent of tax revenues. By the early

"Remember, it's best two out of three."

1990s foreign lenders warned that unless Canadian governments—federal and provincial—got their deficits under control, few would want to invest in government bonds.

One of the major items of government spending was in the new social programs—health care, for example, had become the largest single item—and by the 1990s the question of whether the country could afford the social security and welfare system it had put in place was on the table. The answer seemed to be that it could not, and some changes would have to be made that could square the circle by maintaining service but cutting costs.

Although the slowdown was worldwide, it did underline some of the unique and dangerous weaknesses of the Canadian economy. Canada was highly dependent on trade, but was selling raw or semiprocessed natural resources and importing an increasing amount of manufactured goods, particularly those at the high-technology end. Even with tariff protection it seemed that many manufacturing industries could not compete, even in Canadian markets. During the 1980s Canada ranked last among the G7 countries in productivity growth. At the same time the global economy was changing its shape. Japan had emerged as the second major industrial power, a world leader in high-tech manufacturing. And other countries in Asia were studiously adopting the Japanese model, with the aid of Japanese investment and technology. The nations of Europe had created the European Economic Community (EEC) and were anticipating greater political and economic unity. International trade liberalization was bringing down protective tariff barriers everywhere. It was clear, by the 1980s, that Canada could not remain as it was.

In 1982 Prime Minister Trudeau appointed a royal commission to examine Canada's economic prospects. It reported three years later recommending free trade with the United States. Free trade would protect Canada's export markets—seventy-five percent of our total exports—against potential American protectionism. It would force Canadian industries to improve their performance and become competitive, or disappear. The proposal deeply divided Canadians. Most economists and businesspeople hailed the proposal, arguing that while there would be a loss of jobs in inefficient industries it would increase employment in industries that could compete in the American and international markets. Nationalists argued, as they had in 1891 and 1911, that free trade would not only cost jobs but would also lead to the Americanization of Canada, and ultimately to annexation.

Free trade was adopted by Prime Minister Brian Mulroney, the Conservative leader who had won an overwhelming vic-

The Conservatives were able to ram the free trade bill through the House of Commons despite the vigorous opposition of the Liberal and NDP members. But the Liberal-dominated Senate refused to pass the bill until Mulroney called an election, hoping that the voters would reject the FTA and the government. But Mulroney was returned with a substantial majority of the seats and the bill passed.

tory in the 1984 election. Even before the Commission reported, Mulroney and President Ronald Reagan had agreed to explore freer trade. After two years of intense, and sometimes bitter, negotiations, the Free Trade Agreement (FTA) was approved. The Americans signed it at once; Mulroney took the issue to the people in the 1988 election. The election focused almost entirely on free trade, and the campaign was one of the most emotional in Canadian history. Once again, Mulroney won a decisive victory and the FTA became law on January 1, 1989.

Not long afterwards Canada entered into negotiations with the United States and Mexico to expand the bilateral FTA into a broader North American Free Trade Agreement (NAFTA). An agreement was reached late in 1992 and all that remained was for the three countries to put it into effect. Once again there was strong opposition within Canada among those who feared a mass exodus of industry out of the country due to the availability of cheaper labour in Mexico. But the Mulroney government approved NAFTA, and although in the election of October 1993 the Liberal leader, Jean Chrétien, said he would repudiate the agreement once elected, he changed his mind as prime minister after an hour's talk with President Clinton.

Much less obvious than the changes in the economy have been equally dramatic changes in the nature of the Canadian workforce. Statisticians divide us into two groups: those who produce goods—manufacturing, agriculture, forestry, mining, and construction—and those who provide services—stores, banks, transportation, education and the professions, restaurants, hotels, and government. A century ago about seventy-five percent of the population produced goods; today seventy-five percent provide services.

And the ratio continues to change. Economists preach that Canada must become an increasingly service-oriented economy with an emphasis on the high-technology and knowledge-intensive end of the economy. But the proverbial man or woman on the street is puzzled by the prospect of an economy where almost no one produces goods and we all make our living exchanging services.

This change in the nature of the workforce has also helped to bring more women into the labour market and has enhanced their opportunities, as have affirmative action and pay equity programs. In 1976 men outnumbered women in the "white-collar" workforce by almost two to one. However, between 1976 and 1993 there were two million new white-collar jobs, and sixty-two percent of them went to women, the number increasing to seventy-eight percent between 1988 and 1993. Today men and women are almost equally represented. Over the same period the ratio of women to men in management (nineteen percent to forty-two percent), the professions (forty-four percent to fifty-six percent), and even in science and engineering (seven percent to eighteen percent) has risen dramatically. In addition to the movement for equal participation between men and women at all levels of the economy and equal pay for equal work have been the demands for more day care centres, differential workloads, more flexible work schedules for women with children, and more generous maternity benefits to offset the costs of having a child.

Today the Canadian economy is in the painful process of reconstruction. Worldwide competition is forcing firms everywhere to become "leaner and meaner" by cutting labour costs, improving technology, and expanding markets—or close their doors. At the same time some Canadian natural resource industries are under severe pressure due to falling world prices, international competition, declining resources, or the necessity of adopting stricter and more expensive environmental controls. Tragically, the Atlantic fishing industry had to be virtually closed down for an unspecified length of time because of declining fish stocks; had fishing continued in the same quantities, it was believed that the fish would disappear.

During the early 1990s governments were handicapped by growing deficits, which they were finding difficult to control. And by 1994 interest charges alone on the national debt consumed thirty-four cents of every Canadian tax dollar. Unemployment remained stubbornly high at eleven percent, and in some provinces over ten percent of the people lived on welfare. In the mid-1990s Canadians took little comfort in knowing that most other industrial countries faced some—if not all—of the same problems.

6 The Lawmakers: Parliament and Politicians

CANADIAN PARLIAMENT is an ancient institution whose origins go back to thirteenth-century England and even earlier. It was in English Parliament that the battle was fought between the monarchs and their subjects to determine who would really run the country. The word itself comes from the French word *parler*—to speak or talk—which is what the politicians spend a good deal of their time doing there. But however boisterous or ill-tempered, however serious or playful, whether in Ottawa or the provincial legislatures, this talk is about the policies, programs, and laws that govern our lives. The parliamentary system is not perfect, and while many see room for improvement, few would argue that Canada should adopt a different system.

Democratic governments have an executive and a legislative branch, and the secret to understanding how the system works is to understand the relationship between the two. In the United States the two government branches are quite separate. The president is elected directly by the people. The members of Congress—which consists of the House of Representatives and the Senate—are also directly elected. The president may propose laws, but Congress must pass them. Congress may reject the president's proposals or change them, and the president may reject the laws passed by Congress.

Even if the president and a majority in Congress belong to the same political party, there is no guarantee that his or her proposed laws will be accepted because each member of Congress feels free to vote as he or she chooses. The members of the president's cabinet cannot be members of Congress. Congress must approve the president's appointments to the cabinet, the courts, and other key positions. The principle is the separation of powers, and it is often described as a system of checks and balances. Such a system ensures that neither the executive nor the legislature is able to wield excessive power.

In the Canadian parliamentary system the relationship between the executive and legislative branches is the exact opposite to that of the United States. Instead of a separation there is a fusion of powers. The executive is actually in the legislative branch and, in fact, dominates it. Although in theory the head of the executive is the Governor General, representing the Queen, the real head is the prime minister. The prime minister is not directly elected, but is simply one of the 295 elected members of the House of Commons. He or she becomes prime minister by becoming the elected leader of the party that holds a majority of seats in—or has the confidence of—the House of Commons.

In forming the cabinet, the prime minister attempts to select men and women who represent all provinces, or regions within provinces, possess varying economic and social interests, and are representative of various cultural communities. Each cabinet minister is placed in charge of a department of the government—such as finance, national defence, or immigration. The cabinet as a whole determines the broad lines of government policy, and although members may disagree in cabinet discussions, the principle of collective responsibility is so strong that once the decision is reached all must support it or else resign from the cabinet. Each minister is then given the responsibility of developing the detailed policy for his or her department. Here, the minister relies very heavily on the expertise and advice of the senior civil servants—often called mandarins after

DO NOT FAIL TO HEAR

Mrs. Nellie L. McClung

LECTURE

On Woman Suffrage, Temperance Issues and Things Political.

AN OPEN DISCUSSION IS DESIRED

Mrs. McClung is acknowledged to be one of the foremost platform speakers in the west to-day.

THE TOWN HALL, KILLARNEY

THURSDAY, JUNE THE 18TH

AT EIGHT O'CLOCK SHARP

Reserved Seats 35c. General Admission 25c.

Plan of Hall at Evans' Drug Store.

Nellie McClung was the best known "suffragette" in the battle to secure the vote for women. Although she fought across the country, her greatest battle was in Manitoba. Premier Roblin attacked the movement as one backed only "by men who wear long hair and women who wear short hair." But in 1916 the male fortress fell in Manitoba. Other provinces soon followed and women received the vote in national elections in 1918, although female relatives of soldiers had been allowed to vote in the conscription election of 1917. Women could not vote in Quebec until 1940.

the wise men who once advised the rulers of China!—who, as a result, wield considerable power. The ministers answer all questions about their department in the House of Commons, and introduce and defend their legislation. If the House defeats the proposed legislation on an important subject or explicitly votes "no confidence" in the government, the prime minister and the cabinet must resign. Defeat usually leads to another election, although the Governor General could call on another party leader to form a new government if they could command a majority in the Commons—but this happens very rarely.

The key, therefore, to understanding the parliamentary system is grasping this responsibility of the executive to the elected members in the House of Commons. Nowhere is this responsibility written down, yet it is the most important part of our unwritten Constitution, which we inherited from the United Kingdom and is often described as "responsible government."

The American president appears to be—and is—a very powerful figure. But when it comes to the power to make laws, impose taxes, or make treaties with foreign countries, the president is much less powerful than the Canadian prime minister. When the prime minister and the cabinet reach a decision they know it will be approved because they control a majority in the House of Commons. Party discipline is very strong, and they know that members of the party will not—except on very rare and isolated occasions—vote against them and bring about the defeat of the government.

The Canadian system is certainly stable, except in those rare cases when an election does not give any party a clear majority and the government must depend on the support of the other parties. But many argue that the Canadian system is much less democratic than the American. Although their party connection might be strong, the members of U.S. Congress are free to follow their own convictions whatever the level of pressure exerted by the White House. But the ordinary member—the backbencher—in the Commons is much less free, because voting against the government could result in its defeat. Backbenchers do have an opportunity in the meetings of the party caucus to express their views, and a wise government will listen to them. But when the matter reaches the floor of the House the members of Parliament (MPs) have little or no independence. Indeed, it has been observed that the principle of responsibility of the executive to the legislature should be reversed to read the responsibility or the obligation of the party to support the executive!

Debates in Canadian Parliament, therefore, are much less meaningful than in American Congress. Since the result is usually a forgone conclusion, the debates serve largely as an opportunity for opposition parties to place the government on the defensive. The best opportunity for such debate is in daily question period, when the House of Commons opens each afternoon. Opposition speakers bombard the prime minister and the cabinet with questions about policy and accusations of incompetence. The press is always in full attendance, and the probing that takes place in question period supplies much of the material reported in the newspapers and on television. When question period is over, the press gallery empties and, like the reporters, most ministers and members find better things to do than listen to the long-winded debates that follow.

Demands for changes in Canada's parliamentary system have been growing for many years, and some changes have been made to increase the influence of the backbenchers. Committees of the House of Commons on such matters as finance, foreign affairs, and other government activities have increased in number and have been given more power to scrutinize legislation. These committees have the power to call witnesses and are open to those outside Parliament who are concerned about the legislation in question, and occasionally public consultations are held across the country. Committees frequently suggest alterations or improvements in legislation, but seldom do anything more. Once again, since the membership of the committees—usually seven MPs—reflects the strength of the parties in the House, the government has little to fear in the way of opposition to its policies.

"It's either a new get-tough policy with the provinces, a patriation costume party, or they've been watching too much Shogun during caucus . . ."

The scrum: radio, television, and newspaper reporters patrol the corridors of the Commons to catch party leaders or cabinet ministers as they emerge from a debate or a meeting of the party caucus. The manoeuvre resembles a scrimmage in rugger—thus the word scrum.

Cartoonist Roy Peterson pictures Trudeau and his cabinet preparing for the war of the words as they emerge from a caucus meeting.

Roy Peterson, *Vancouver Sun*, September 7, 1980.

The most frequent proposal to free the backbenchers from strict party discipline is to allow more free votes. If this were the case, only on matters of critical importance to the government's policy—the budget, for example—should defeat mean resignation. Occasionally a government has stated that all members are free to vote according to conscience—on abortion, for example—and the vote would not be taken as a vote of nonconfidence. But such occasions usually arise because the government either has no policy or cannot persuade the party caucus to adopt a position, as occurred with an abortion law after the famous Morgentaler case. In an article called "Call Off The Party" (*Policy Options*, March 1989), David Kilgour, then a Conservative MP from Edmonton, argued that making a free vote the rule rather than the exception would make the Canadian government more democratic.

> *The constituents of both provincial and federal legislators would be the real winners if party discipline were to be loosened. Private members from both government and opposition benches could then take positions on government bills and other matters based on pleasing constituents, instead of their respective party hierarchies.*
>
> *At present, few government and opposition MPs have any real opportunity to put their constituents first in votes in the House of Commons. Real power is concentrated in the hands of three [five in 1993] party leaderships. Canadian democracy itself would benefit substantially if we put our present mind-numbing party discipline where it belongs—in the history books.*

Ironically, a year after writing the article, David Kilgour was expelled from the Conservative caucus, personally attacked by the prime minister, and forced to sit on the Opposition side of the Commons when he voted against the Mulroney government's goods and services tax (GST).

There are also those who argue that the way we run our elections does not even guarantee that the House of Commons reflects the popular will. Very rarely—indeed only twice since

Not all that much has changed since Laurier's day. Patronage—a job, a contract, the location of a government building—is still part of politics. As Israel Tarte, one of Laurier's cabinet ministers, said, "elections are not won with prayers."

Toronto News.

1945—has the governing party won fifty percent of the popular vote. In other words, a majority in Parliament does not really mean rule by the majority. This is because of our single member ridings and multiparty system. For election purposes, the country is divided up into 295 constituencies, or ridings. The major parties run candidates in all or most of the ridings. The candidate with the most votes wins. Mathematically, a party could win 100% of the seats with only 295 votes more than its opponents by winning each seat by one vote.

There are less theoretical examples. In the 1987 election in New Brunswick the Liberal party won every seat in the legislature with sixty percent of the vote. That meant that forty percent of the people of the province were without a voice in government. In the 1980 federal election over twenty percent of the voters in Saskatchewan, Alberta, and British Columbia voted Liberal. But only one Liberal was elected. In 1993 the Liberals under Jean Chrétien received only forty-one percent of the votes, but they won 178 or sixty percent of the seats in the Commons and formed a "majority" government.

Parties also argue that victory gives them a mandate to implement their program. Consider the election of 1988: Most people felt the critical issue was free trade with the United States, which was supported by Brian Mulroney and the Conservatives and opposed by the other parties. Mulroney won a majority of the seats with forty-three percent of the vote and passed the free trade legislation. Would free trade have been approved in a national referendum where everybody could have voted on the issue? If not, can we really claim that we are ruled by the majority?

Elections, which in Canada must occur at least every five years, lie at the heart of the democratic process. But running a political party, with its large staff of organizers and propagandists, and fighting a campaign is a multimillion-dollar operation. And it is critically important that the battle be fought on a level playing field. Until relatively recently, however, there were no limits on how much money parties or candidates could spend on an election campaign, and the field was tilted towards the party that could raise the most money, usually from large corporations. However, in 1974, the Trudeau government enacted legislation that limited the amount parties and candidates could spend during the campaign, tightened the controls on political donations, and provided that some of each candidate's expenses would be payed by the government. Most provinces also have passed laws controlling election expenses. No limits were imposed, however, on how much parties could spend up to the moment an election was called.

Moreover, the law did not prevent organizations other than political parties from spending money during a campaign supporting or denouncing the policies favoured by one party or the other. In 1983, however, the law was changed to prohibit such activities. The National Citizens' Coalition, a supposedly nonpartisan but strong free enterprise association, argued in court that the law violated the freedom of expression guaranteed by the Charter of Rights and Freedoms. The judge agreed and the law was declared invalid. As a result there are no limits on such expenditures, and during the 1988 campaign organizations supporting—and some opposing—free trade spent millions of dollars on newspaper and television advertising. Until a new law is passed that will not be considered a violation of freedom of expression, rich and powerful organizations are perfectly free to campaign on the sidelines of the not-so-level playing field.

The Senate, the upper house in the legislature, has little to do with the electoral process. When the Fathers of Confederation were designing the 1867 Constitution there was considerable debate as to whether the senators should be elected or appointed, and whether each province should have equal representation in the Senate. There was little support for an elected Senate and the large colonies refused to consider equal representation. Senators were to be appointed for life by the prime minister, and regions—the Atlantic provinces, Quebec, Ontario, and ultimately the West—would have equal representation. Except for its inability to change legislation concerning money—for example, taxing or spending—the Senate was given powers equal to the House of Commons.

If the expectations were that the Senate would, as Sir John A. Macdonald said, be a house of "sober second thought" that could keep a check on the popularly elected Commons, or that it would serve as a protector of regional/provincial interests, neither ideal proved accurate. Even Macdonald admitted that an appointed Senate would "never set itself in opposition to the deliberate and understood wishes of the people," and except on rare occasions the Senate has not stood in the way of the Commons. Party allegiance has proven far stronger in the Senate than protecting provincial

Only in rare and exceptional circumstances has the Senate defied the will of the House of Commons. One such case occurred in 1912 when the Senate, dominated by the Liberals after Laurier's fifteen years in power, rejected the Conservatives' bill to give Britain $35 million to build three battleships. The Conservatives had won the 1911 election, partly on that issue, but the Senate nevertheless sent the bill back to the House with the message that "This House is not justified in giving assent to the Bill until it is submitted to the judgement of the country."

Toronto News.

---

interests. It was not long before the role of the Senate was simply to provide a convenient source of patronage that the prime minister could use to reward faithful party servants. Surprisingly, there has never been a strong movement to abolish the Senate, although few outside the Senate would have fought very hard to keep it.

During the discussions about constitutional reform in the past thirty years, however, there has been a renewed interest in a reformed Senate. The explanation lies in what some see as the unequal representation of the various parts of Canada in the Commons. Because of their large populations, Ontario and

Quebec elect 174 of the 295 members of the Commons, while the West elects only eighty-six members—fewer even than Ontario's ninety-nine—and the Atlantic provinces elect only thirty-two. Toronto itself has more seats (twenty-three) than any of the Atlantic provinces, Manitoba and Saskatchewan, and only two less than Alberta. Not only are there more members from Ontario and Quebec than from any other region, there are also, as a result, many more Quebec and Ontario members in the cabinet. Westerners in particular believe that national governments inevitably pursue policies that favour the large central provinces, and can readily find examples to support their argument—such as Prime Minister Trudeau's national energy policy in 1980.

A reformed Senate appeared to be a solution to this regional imbalance in the Commons. By the late 1980s the western provinces had endorsed the principle of a Triple-E Senate: it would have Equal representation from each province, with Elected senators, and its powers would be Effective, although what those powers would be was not clear. An opinion poll in 1989 revealed that a majority of Canadians, except in Quebec, approved of an elected Senate. Another poll in 1992 showed that over fifty percent in the West, forty-four percent in the Maritimes, thirty-eight percent in Ontario, and twenty-seven percent in Quebec supported a Triple-E Senate. During the constitutional discussions in the early 1990s Ontario and Quebec opposed a Triple-E Senate, but finally gave in when it became clear that unless they agreed the western provinces would not agree to other reforms.

Finally, in the Charlottetown Accord forged in the summer of 1992, all governments agreed to a version of the Triple-E Senate. Six senators were to be elected from each province, and could be elected by the legislature of the province. Some key federal government appointments were to be subject to Senate approval. The Accord also gave the Senate a veto over any tax changes affecting natural resources, an issue of major concern to the western provinces. The Senate, it seemed, had gained a new lease on life. But, as we shall see, the Canadian people rejected the Charlottetown Accord in a national referendum, and the proposal died. However, it was not surprising that in the October 25, 1993, election the Reform Party, led by Preston Manning, a fervent supporter of the Triple-E Senate, won fifty of the seventy-two seats in the three most western provinces. When and if constitutional reform is back on the national agenda, so too will be the Triple-E Senate.

On the whole Canadians seem reasonably content with their parliamentary system. An international survey in 1994 revealed that forty-four percent approved of it and thirty-five percent disapproved, whereas in the United States and Britain the figures were reversed. However, Canadians had little faith in their politicians. In the same poll over eighty percent stated that they believe nothing or almost nothing that politicians say (*Globe and Mail,* 16 March 1994). Skepticism in a democracy is healthy; but such a high level of distrust for our politicians suggests that many Canadians believe that the object of party politics is to win and keep power, not to serve the public interest. Apparently the parliamentary system is trustworthy, but the politicians are not.

7 Ottawa and the Provinces

THE HARSH REALITIES of geography and history combined to make Canada a federal rather than a unitary state, where legislative and financial powers were divided between one central, or national, government and ten provincial governments.

As discussed in chapter three, by the 1860s both internal and external circumstances dictated that the British colonies in North America should consider some form of union to solve the problems they all faced. After lengthy discussions, the Fathers of Confederation decided to create a new country that would embrace the geographic expanse of British North America.

The threat of American expansion and the necessity of developing a strong economy suggested to some that all the colonies should unite under one government. But no colony was prepared to submerge itself completely in the new nation. Indeed, it was the inability of the French and the English to live under one government in the Canadas that sparked the federation movement. Paradoxically, in fact, Confederation was a response to the demand in the Canadas for a divorce and subsequent remarriage under a new contract. While a unitary state seemed impossible, the question was, what kind of federal system could best meet the conflicting demands of unity and diversity?

The Fathers of Confederation were not political philosophers with grand theories, but pragmatic politicians concerned with the day-to-day functions that the national and provincial governments should perform. The national government clearly needed the economic and financial muscle to weld the provinces together, build and manage the national economy, and defend the country. The provinces could safely be left with control over the social, cultural, and to some extent, business life of the local communities. They were given control over education, hospitals, local roads and railroads, local governments, and the administration of justice. Their powers of taxation were limited to direct taxation, largely through granting licences since the income tax had not yet been invented. But provinces did retain control of their public lands and natural resources.

Everything not given to the provinces was left to the national, or federal, government. In so doing, the Fathers of Confederation explicitly rejected the model of American federal constitution. The American colonies had been afraid of a strong central government and had given it limited powers and retained everything else—the residual powers—for themselves. But the Canadians believed that powerful states and a weak centre had led to the Civil War then raging south of the border, and were determined not to make the same mistake. As a result, they gave the federal government the residual power—the power "to make laws for the Peace, Order, and good Government of Canada in relation to all matters not . . . assigned exclusively to the Legislatures of the provinces . . ."

To make doubly sure of establishing a strong central government, the Fathers provided, "for greater certainty," a list of some of the powers to be exclusively exercised by the federal government: all forms of taxation, the regulation of trade and commerce, money and banking, interprovincial transportation, defence, the criminal law (which in the United States had been given to the states), and the appointment of judges in provincial courts. The federal government also appointed the provincial lieutenant-governors—then regarded as important officers, who would keep their eye on the activities of the provincial governments, and had the

A LITTLE TOO MUCH OF THE WHIP.

Macdonald and the provinces, as pictured by the political cartoonist, J.W. Bengough.

Grip, June 16, 1883.

---

power to "disallow" provincial legislation. Clearly, as the Fathers intended and admitted, they had created a highly centralized federal system, where the federal government possessed much more power than the provinces.

But the intentions of the Fathers were never fully realized. The history of Canadian federalism has been one not of continuous federal supremacy, but of a constant battle between Ottawa and the provinces. At times—particularly during the two world wars—power shifted dramatically to the centre; at other times the balance of power shifted to the provinces. Today the provinces are far more powerful and the central government much weaker than the Fathers of Confederation could ever have imagined.

There were many reasons why the federal government did not establish and maintain its dominance over the provinces. Loyalty to the provinces remained strong—stronger among many people than to the new country itself. Indeed, some scholars maintain that it was only the exceptional circumstances in the 1860s that persuaded many colonial politicians to accept the strong central government, and once those circumstances changed they no longer saw any need for strength at the centre. Strong provincial premiers, such as Oliver Mowat in Ontario, found it politically beneficial to fight for provincial "rights." (Most still do.) Mowat and others successfully challenged the federal power of disallowance because it violated their right to self-government, and insisted that the lieutenant-governor was simply a representative of the Crown in the provincial government and not a federal agent.

The Courts, which were responsible for determining whether a certain power lay within federal or provincial jurisdiction, played a critical role in defining the relationship between the two levels of government. The Supreme Court of Canada interpreted federal powers broadly, but the final court of appeal was the Judicial Committee in London, England. From the 1880s until appeals to the Judicial Committee were abolished in 1949, the British court continuously and enthusiastically decided in favour of the provinces and reduced federal powers to a shadow of what the Fathers had intended. By 1949 the federal Constitution was not so much what was written in the BNA Act in 1867 as what the Judicial Committee had decided during the intervening years.

More fundamentally, centralization failed because both Ontario and Quebec were too large and powerful in relation to the national government. In the United States there were at first thirteen states, and then twenty, and then fifty, and never has one or two or three states dominated the political or economic scene. But in Canada, Ontario and Quebec virtually *were* Canada in 1867, with seventy-seven percent of the population, and even today, despite the growth of the West, they contain sixty percent of the Canadian population. It was difficult for the federal government to adopt policies opposed by governments who claimed to speak for such a large percentage of the people, even though Ottawa could claim to speak for 100 percent of the country.

Moreover, much of the economic development of the twentieth century lay in fields and public lands owned and controlled by the provincial governments: pulp and paper, minerals, oil and gas, and hydroelectricity. Although small in population, Alberta and British Columbia also gained the economic and financial independence and clout to stand up to Ottawa after 1945. Finally, not only do the provinces have equal access to the lucrative income tax fields, but apart from the banks they control the most important financial institutions: stock exchanges, trust and mortgage companies, credit unions, and insurance companies. By the 1960s all the provinces were developing their own "province-building" economic policy, often in conflict with each other or the objectives of the federal government. As a result, most, if not all, economists would agree that the central government today has less power over the economy than that of any other industrialized country.

Perhaps even more remarkable, throughout the history of Canada, has been the changing function of the state. Until the twentieth century the ordinary Canadian lived largely independent of the government, including paying little, if anything, in taxes. A century ago the family was responsible for the sick, the aged, and the unemployed; if necessary, these burdens fell on local churches or charities, or, in extreme cases, local or provincial governments. But all that changed as Canada became an urban and industrialized society. Today there are few aspects of our lives that are not regulated, controlled, or paid for by the local, provincial, and national governments. Public education from kindergarten through university, health care, old age pensions, unemployment insurance and social welfare, subsidized public transit, and public housing are all twentieth-century inventions.

Most of these new functions of government—mass education, social security, and welfare—fell within provincial jurisdiction, and in its decision on the distribution of powers in the Constitution, the Judicial Committee in Britain, adopting the metaphor of "watertight compartments," made it clear

"I see, I see," Madame Moira hesitated. "I see horses and buggies and bustles and crinolines, and petticoats—and all manner of quaint old-fashioned things. "That," explained Mr. King, "is the British North America Act."

It was not generally known in 1935 that Mackenzie King was a spiritualist who remained in touch with the world beyond through visions and consulting the departed (such as Laurier) by table tapping, consulting fortune tellers, and attending seances. Whether the cartoonist knew it or not, it did not take messages from beyond to demonstrate that by 1935 the 1867 Constitution needed to be overhauled.

Montreal Standard, January 5, 1935.

---

that they would stay there. As the provinces' responsibilities increased—provincial and municipal spending increased from $25 million a year in 1900 to $700 million a year by 1929—so did the importance of the provincial governments in the minds of the people. But the provinces, particularly the smaller and poorer ones, did not have the financial resources to pay for these new social functions, and the Depression of the 1930s revealed that even the richer provinces could not support the unemployed. Moreover, it seemed appropriate that all Canadians should enjoy the same benefits wherever they lived.

As a result, during and after World War II the federal and provincial governments embarked on a long and sometimes stormy journey towards the social security system we have today. The provinces agreed to constitutional amendments that gave the federal government power over unemployment insurance and old age security. A system called "shared-cost" programs was used to get around the distribution of powers in the Constitution and implement national health, hospital, and medical care. The federal government agreed to pay half the cost if the provinces agreed to certain conditions and would administer the programs. The federal government also agreed to pay half the cost of provincial welfare programs and of university education, with very few conditions. In 1993 the federal government transferred $30 billion to the provinces for provincial health care, welfare, and postsecondary education.

"Equalization payments" to the poorer provinces were another invention of the postwar era. The Depression of the 1930s had revealed, more starkly than ever before, that there were enormous differences in wealth among the provinces and, therefore, in the level of services they could provide. Not only were there differences in natural resources, but also most of the financial and industrial companies were located in Central Canada, where the companies and their highly paid employees were taxed even though their money had been made all across the country. The disparities, therefore, seemed not only un-Canadian but unfair. In 1957 the federal government decided to provide additional funds to the poorer provinces to bring their governments' incomes closer to the level of the richer provinces. These "equalization" payments meant, in fact, that taxes received from residents of the richer provinces—Ontario, Alberta, and British Columbia—would go to help the residents of the others. The principle of equalization was written into the new Constitution in 1982. In

1993 those payments, which could be regarded as another form of social security, totaled $8 billion.

During the boom years of the 1960s only gloomy pessimists suggested that the social security system was too rich for our blood. But as early as 1977—with costs soaring, particularly for health and welfare—the federal government began to place a ceiling on its contributions, which in effect meant that unless the provinces could control costs they would be forced to pay a greater share. However, with high unemployment in the 1980s and 1990s, and with an aging population, it seemed impossible to control health and welfare costs. But by the 1990s, as all governments faced staggering deficits (and the taxpayers were going underground if they could), it seemed clear that the social security system would have to be redesigned in order to survive. Exactly how was the question.

The vast array of taxes necessary to pay for the revolution in government expenditures was also a twentieth-century invention: the personal income tax, corporation income tax, sales and gasoline tax, and the goods and services tax. The share of the total wealth produced in the country—or the Gross Domestic Product (GDP)—that is taxed and spent by the government has increased dramatically. There are no accurate figures for 1867, but an educated guess would be that the government spent less than five percent of the GDP. Sixty years ago the figure was only sixteen percent. Today it is over fifty percent.

Of these taxes by far the most important are the direct taxes, particularly the personal income tax, which was first introduced in 1917 by the federal government as a "temporary" tax to pay for World War I. And between the wars most provinces introduced the personal income tax to pay for the expensive new functions they had assumed. During World War II the federal government took over exclusive control of the direct tax fields. After the war Ottawa hoped to establish one national direct tax system and offered to "rent" the income tax fields from the provinces. But Quebec and Ontario refused, and by the 1960s the noble and sensible attempt was

Most taxpayers know little of the war between Ottawa and the provinces over dividing the tax pie. They know only that taxes always seem to go up and, despite the promises, never come down.

Reprinted with permission—*The Toronto Star* Syndicate.

given up. Ottawa agreed to collect all the income taxes—except for Quebec—but each province was free to add as much as it wished to the federal income tax. By 1990 the federal government raised fifty-two percent of its revenue from personal income taxes (much of it was transferred to the provinces for shared-cost programs and equalization payments), and the provinces raised twenty-five percent. Both levels of government accused the other of taking too much while the groaning taxpayers prayed that they would leave a little room for them.

Federal-provincial negotiations over shared-cost programs and tax sharing were far from amicable. But the strongest opposition to the intervention of the federal government and the expansion of its activities, as well as the loudest demands for a greater share of the taxes, came from Quebec. By the 1960s the government of Quebec, supported by ultranationalists and indirectly by bomb-throwing separatists, was insisting on a radical revision of the federal Constitution, with vastly greater powers for "l'état du Québec." This was but another chapter in the history of the conflict of cultures to which we must now turn, even though the last chapter cannot yet be written.

8 The Conflict of Cultures

NOT LONG AFTER CONFEDERATION in 1867, a leading French-Canadian politician wrote: "English and French, we climb by a double flight of stairs towards the destinies reserved for us on this continent, without knowing each other, without meeting each other, and without even seeing each other, except on the landing of politics." The British conquest was more than a century old then. English and French had lived together for over 100 years, but had not found a common nationality. Today there are many French Canadians, or Québécois, who believe that the conquest of 1763 must be undone, and that the province of Quebec must become an independent state. This conflict of cultures continues to be one of the most serious problems facing modern Canada.

The survival of the French Canadians has often been described as a miracle. In 1763 they were a crushed people, numbering only 60,000, many of whose leaders left for France on the morrow of defeat. Even without the benefit of mass immigration from France, the French Canadians today number six million. The vast majority live in the province of Quebec, which is mainly French-speaking (although the English-speaking minority of over half a million wields considerable economic and financial power). But French Canadians have also spread beyond the borders of their homeland. Almost half of New Brunswick is French; and Ontario, Manitoba, Nova Scotia, and Prince Edward Island have significant French-Canadian communities.

Survival or *la survivance* became the battlecry of French Canada after the conquest. *Je me souviens*—I remember—was the maxim. The weapons in the battle for cultural survival were the French language and the Roman Catholic religion, both guaranteed by the British in the Quebec Act of 1774. The army was provided by a high birthrate: French Canadians spoke of *la revanche du berceau*—the revenge of the cradle. The battleground was usually the "landing of politics."

At first the conflict was fought in what is now the province of Quebec. After the American Revolution, English-speaking immigrants from the thirteen colonies had entered the colony, either to settle the land or to engage in trade and commerce. It was not long before the English minority and the French majority were engaged in battle. In the economic field, the English wanted to develop trade and commerce and to levy taxes to build harbours and canals; the French lived largely on the land and objected to paying taxes to assist the commercial practices of the English-speaking city dwellers. In politics, the English enjoyed positions on the British governor's appointed council, where they could exercise great influence and power; the French had a large majority in the elected assembly and believed that the governor should listen to their advice and not to that of the English-speaking merchants and bankers.

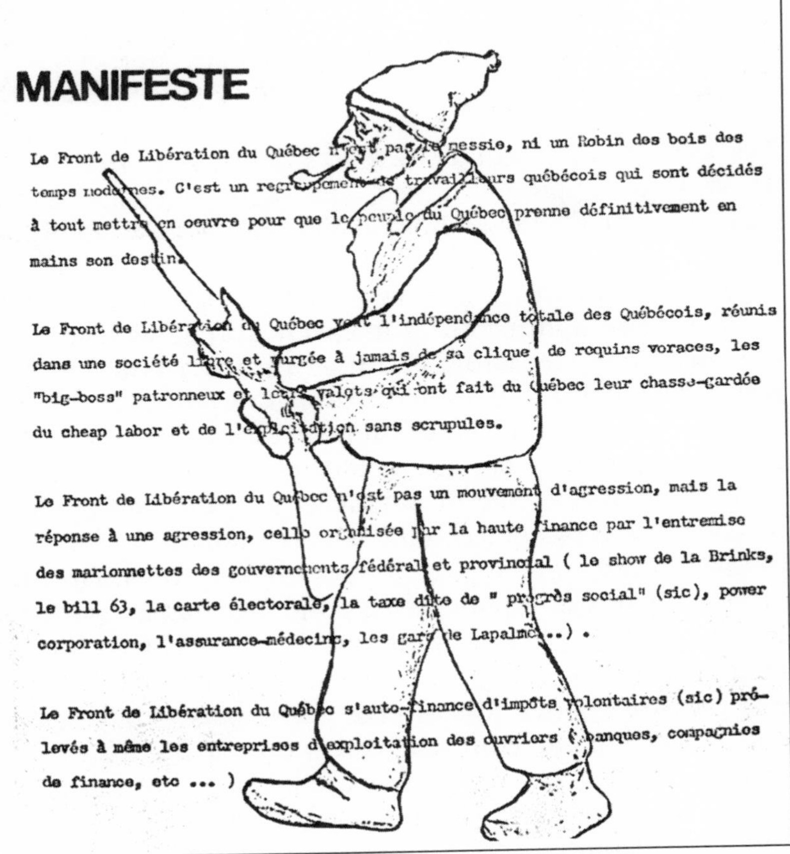

front de libération du québec

MANIFESTE

Le Front de Libération du Québec n'est pas le messie, ni un Robin des bois des temps modernes. C'est un regroupement de travailleurs québécois qui sont décidés à tout mettre en oeuvre pour que le peuple du Québec prenne définitivement en mains son destin.

Le Front de Libération du Québec veut l'indépendance totale des Québécois, réunis dans une société libre et purgée à jamais de sa clique de requins voraces, les "big-boss" patronneux et leurs valets qui ont fait du Québec leur chasse-gardée du cheap labor et de l'exploitation sans scrupules.

Le Front de Libération du Québec n'est pas un mouvement d'agression, mais la réponse à une agression, celle organisée par la haute finance par l'entremise des marionnettes des gouvernements fédéral et provincial (le show de la Brinks, le bill 63, la carte électorale, la taxe dite de " progrès social" (sic), power corporation, l'assurance-médecine, les gars de Lapalme...) .

Le Front de Libération du Québec s'auto-finance d'impôts volontaires (sic) prélevés à même les entreprises d'exploitation des ouvriers (banques, compagnies de finance, etc ...)

The "patriote" of 1837 was used as the symbol of the revolutionary Front de Libération du Québec (FLQ) in the famous October crisis of 1970.

Unable to win on the political battlefield, in 1837 Louis Joseph Papineau, the French leader in the assembly, roused his followers, the Patriotes, to arms. At the same time, for some of the same reasons, William Lyon Mackenzie led an uprising in Upper Canada. Although there were many reasons for the ill-fated rebellions, Lord Durham, who was sent to investigate, concluded the rebellion in Quebec was the result of racial conflict. In his famous report he wrote, "I found two nations warring within the bosom of a single state: I found a struggle, not of principles, but of race." Believing that the French were backward, and the English merchants progressive, Durham maintained that the only answer to the racial conflict was to swamp the French population. Unite Upper and Lower Canada, he argued, and in a short time the combined English-speaking population of the two colonies would outnumber the French. Assimilation of the French would then only be a matter of time.

As Durham pointed out, there were also good economic arguments for the union, and the British government followed his advice and united the colonies. But Durham's attack served only to make French Canadians even more determined to maintain their culture; to attach themselves even more firmly to their language, religion, and the values of their rural agricultural society; and to make them impress *je me souviens* even more indelibly on their children. And in the assembly the French-Canadian political leaders were quick to oppose any move that smacked of inequality or seemed to threaten their survival. The elaborate game of chess in the assembly gradually paralysed the government of the colony and was one of the major reasons for Confederation in 1867.

Confederation once again divided the two Canadas, this time into the provinces of Ontario and Quebec: the former overwhelmingly English-speaking, and the latter overwhelmingly French. The two were then united along with the other colonies in the Canadian federation. Far from reflecting a desire on the part of the English and the French to live more closely together, Confederation reflected the fact that they could not live together under one government.

The federal union was based on the hope that French and English could live in peaceful coexistence if there was nothing to fight over. The Constitution, therefore, gave to the provinces all matters of special concern to each cultural group, while the federal government was given responsibility for broad national policies that did not involve religious, linguistic, or cultural interests. The Constitution also guaranteed the educational rights of the Protestant English minority in Quebec and the Roman Catholic minority in Ontario, and the use of the French and English languages in the Canadian Parliament and the Quebec legislature. Now, the Fathers of Confederation hoped, the "landing of politics" would be free from the battles of the past, and French Canadians would no longer be obsessed with survival, for although they were a minority in Canada, they had control of their own government in the province of Quebec.

These happy expectations were never realized. The ink was scarcely dry on the British North America Act of 1867 when the French Canadians found that the conflict of cultures could not be removed from national life. Moving beyond the borders of Quebec, French Canadians soon realized that Canada was basically an English-speaking country. They encountered an alien and often hostile culture that refused to provide schools where their children could be educated in their own language and religion, and forced them to live and work in English if they wished to succeed. Even the province of Manitoba—where there was a large French-speaking population, and where French-speaking language rights had been guaranteed in 1870 when Manitoba entered Confederation—abolished French schools and ended the right of members to speak French in the legislature in 1890.

The importance of Quebec to French Canadians was reinforced by the realization that they were often powerless in Ottawa. This point was powerfully driven home when in 1885 the Métis rebelled against the Canadian government, which had been guilty of seriously mismanaging Western

A RIEL UGLY POSITION.

Macdonald's dilemma as seen by a contemporary critic, J.W. Bengough. *Grip*, August 29, 1885.

Canada. When the rebellion was crushed and Louis Riel, the Métis leader, surrendered, English Canada demanded that Riel be executed. French Canada asked for mercy, pleading that he was fighting for the survival of a people and arguing, with some validity, that he was insane. Pressed by English Canadians, the government followed the letter of the law despite the almost unanimous chorus from Quebec demanding that Riel's life be spared.

Fourteen years later it was again made clear that French Canada's voice could be drowned out in Ottawa. English Canada demanded that Canadian troops be sent to assist the British in the Boer War in South Africa; French Canada argued that the war was of no concern to Canada and opposed participation. But even Sir Wilfrid Laurier, a French-Canadian prime minister, had to bow to the loud demands from the English-Canadian majority.

From these crises and these defeats—for every crisis was considered a defeat—French Canada learned a painful lesson. National politics *could* centre on racial issues and divide French and English Canadians along racial lines. When that happened, the minority was powerless. The lesson seemed clear. As Henri Bourassa—a brilliant Quebec nationalist who believed in a bicultural Canada—put it, French Canadians were like the Indians who had no rights or power once they left the reservation. Quebec was the French Canadians' reservation. Only there were they a majority; only there could they remain French. *La survivance* remained the touchstone of French Canadian life. And for many the dream of a separate state free from English domination had been reawakened.

A number of setbacks made the dream more frequent and powerful during the twentieth century. In both world wars, the English and the French differed sharply over the extent of Canada's participation. In both cases the English majority won and Canadians were forced to serve overseas. Also, French-language schools outside Quebec were repeatedly attacked and weakened, as many English Canadians seemed to accept Lord Durham's view that assimilation was the answer to the "problem" of French Canada. Even in Quebec itself, English increasingly became the language of business, a language the French *had* to learn to get ahead. Canada might be a nation of two languages and two cultures, but it was clear that it was the French alone who would be bilingual and bicultural.

The old policy of survival had relied in part on isolation from English Canada. In the twentieth century, however, this isolation became increasingly impossible. By 1900 Canada was entering a period of rapid industrialization. Rich forest and mineral resources, abundant supplies of hydroelectric power, the excellent seaports of Quebec and Montreal, and a large supply of inexpensive labour led to the growth of industries in Quebec. There was a flood of labour from the farms to the cities, and the old rural isolation was no longer possible. French Canada had become part of the commercial and industrial life of North America.

But the factories and cities that accompanied the rapid industrialization of Quebec also represented a threat to *la survivance;* they were breeding grounds for new kinds of English–French hostility. The owners and managers of the new industries were not French Canadians, but English-Canadian, American, and British capitalists. Rural French Canada had not built up large amounts of capital for investment, and the government of Quebec itself encouraged foreign and English-Canadian investment. Moreover, the Quebec educational system, run by the Roman Catholic Church, had emphasized the classics, religion, and the humanities—all guardians of culture—but had not trained people to be technicians, businesspeople, and scientists.

Thus, in their own province, French Canadians became the hewers of wood and the drawers of water in an urban and industrial society dominated by others. By the 1960s French Canadians were the most poorly paid workers within Quebec, earning even less than new immigrants from Europe. Their standard of living was ten percent lower than that of the average Canadian, and twenty percent lower than in the neighbouring province of Ontario. Consequently, the province's population growth was shrinking as French Canadians emigrated to other provinces where they could earn higher wages.

By the 1950s the province of Quebec was ripe for radical social and economic change. From the universities, the press, and the trade unions came a flood of criticism about the state of affairs in Quebec. Most of the criticism was directed at the provincial government itself. Conservative French-Canadian politicians, wedded to the old ways and values and dominated by the concern for survival, were blamed for selling the province out to foreign capitalists, and accused of enforcing antilabour policies and of turning their backs on social reform. The educational system, which the government left largely in the hands of the Church, was blamed for not adequately preparing young French Canadians to participate fully in a modern society. Gérard Filion, a prominent French Canadian, assessed the problem and assigned responsibility:

> *Labour drawn to the cities since the last war (1945) came from the countryside and had grade school education, that is, at most Grade 7. These workers landed into a technological civilization without general education and without technical training . . . for the educational system we have given ourselves and for which we are alone responsible, inevitably led to a scorn for economic things and an exaltation of so-called cultural values. It was not the Americans, it was not the English-Canadians, it was not even the English-speaking Quebeckers who inflicted on us for 100 years the education system we had. It is the French-Canadian society which gave itself this system, with the consequences we observe today.*

But English Canadians were not blameless. English was the working language of the new urban, industrial, and commercial society, and French Canadians were handicapped by having to use their second language in their work. Business practices and organization reflected the Anglo-Saxon and not the French mind and character. Large companies were often too eager to exploit the natural and human resources of the province, with too little concern for the welfare of the community.

Discontent mounted during the 1950s. Finally, in 1960, the old politicians of the Union Nationale party were swept out by a Liberal party that had adopted a policy of widespread

Mr. Lapointe: "Once more against the walls, dear friends."

Since 1944 Quebec had been ruled by Premier Maurice Duplessis and the Union Nationale party. Duplessis had built a powerful alliance of conservative forces, including the Roman Catholic Church and big business, and portayed himself as the defender of the Québécois against the designs of the government in Ottawa to destroy provincial rights. Within Quebec Duplessis seemed invulnerable, and like others before it this attempt to defeat him in the election of 1956 failed. In 1960, however, a year after Duplessis died, the fortress fell.

Winnipeg Free Press.

---

reform. What followed has been called the "Quiet Revolution." The educational system was first taken away from the Church and then radically reformed. Other institutions, such as hospitals, were also placed under the control of the state. New social legislation, progressive labour laws, and political reforms were quickly passed. Long accustomed to casting scorn on what they regarded as backward Quebec, English Canadians were quick to applaud the signs of progress and reform. Their applause soon became muted, however, when it became clear that the internal revolution in Quebec would demand great changes in Canada itself.

Without deserting the old motto, *je me souviens*, the Québécois, as they began to call themselves, insisted that in the future they be *maîtres chez nous*—masters in our own house. Quebec, they argued, was not a province like the others. In the cultural sense it was a nation, which, like other nations, had its own culture and history, its own language and institutions, and its own government. Quebec was not a province, it was *l'état du Québec*. As such, it was argued that within the federal system, Quebec should have "special status," with vastly increased powers over the economy and social policy and a much larger slice of the tax pie to pay for them. Some nationalists went further and argued that the only solution to Quebec's place in the Canadian federal state was, in fact, to separate and form an independent state.

By the mid-1960s, as a few militant separatists bombed federal government buildings, Prime Minister Lester B. Pearson's government made some attempts to respond to the demands from Quebec. The provinces were given a larger share of the taxes; Quebec was allowed to "opt out" of some of the new shared-cost programs; and Pearson appointed a Royal Commission to examine the whole issue of biculturalism and bilingualism in Canada. But the concessions did nothing to dampen nationalist demands in Quebec, where, in 1966, a new government was elected that spoke of "*deux nations*," and promised "equality or independence."

There were French Canadians in Quebec, however, who opposed the nationalists, believed that extreme nationalism everywhere became an evil force, and thought that an independent Quebec run by ultranationalists would be disaster for the Québécois. Pierre Trudeau, who entered federal politics in 1965 to combat the nationalists, was one such French Canadian.

Three years later, when Pearson resigned, the Liberals elected Trudeau as his successor. The new prime minister believed that if French Canadians could feel at home everywhere in Canada the separatist appeal would be less attractive. He passed the Official Languages Act, which made French and English the official languages of Canada, equal in status throughout the federal government. Federal civil servants were encouraged to become bilingual so that French

"It's a great success – eight percent of them learn to swim."
CIVIL SERVICE
TOTAL IMMERSION SECOND LANGUAGE ATTEMPTS

There was intense opposition to the policy of bilingualism in many parts of Canada. Moreover, there were many who doubted that the program was a success in Ottawa itself. In 1978, the official responsible for supervising the program declared that he would give the government a C plus. After a decade's experience, only ten percent of the civil servants who graduated from language school, he said, could in fact work in the French language. But as time passed it was increasingly true that in the upper ranks of the civil service everyone could at least be understood when English or French was spoken.

Canadians could work in their own language. Quebeckers were selected for more important positions in the cabinet and the civil service, as evidence that Ottawa, too, was a place they could succeed. And Trudeau encouraged the provinces, with limited success, to support more French-language schools for francophone minorities and more French-language teaching in English-Canadian schools. The Trudeau government also poured more money into Quebec—and other poor provinces—to promote economic development, raise the standard of living, and undermine the economic discontent that fed the nationalist movement. But Trudeau was not prepared to consider the radical redistribution of powers and taxes demanded by Quebec, nor to acknowledge any form of "special status." Trudeau's Quebec, whatever its history and culture, was a province like the others.

In 1968, when Trudeau became prime minister, the democratic separatists in Quebec came together under René Lévesque to form the Parti Québécois. A prominent member of the Liberal cabinet in Quebec from 1960 to 1966, Lévesque had become convinced that the only answer to the question, "what does Quebec want?" was, as he said, Quebec's political independence. But to reduce the costs of independence he concluded that an independent Quebec would need to remain in an economic union with Canada. His policy was known as sovereignty-association—political sovereignty for Quebec with an economic association with the rest of Canada. Lévesque also argued that Quebec needed much more radical and nationalistic social, cultural, and economic reforms than those advocated by the provincial Liberals. The combination of his fervent nationalism, radical policies, and personal magnetism made the Parti Québécois, the *péquistes* as they were called, a formidable political force.

The eyes of the country were on Quebec as the province went to the polls on April 29, 1970. Basically, the contest was between the Liberals, under Robert Bourassa, a staunch believer in federalism *if* provincial powers and revenues could be vastly expanded, and René Lévesque, who asked the voters to say *oui* to a separate state. English Canada was unanimous in its support of the Liberals, and was alarmed by the pre-election polls that revealed *péquiste* strength. Business leaders and federalists predicted economic catastrophe for an independent Quebec, and a fleet of Brinks trucks dramatically moved securities from Montreal to Toronto to underline the danger.

The Liberals won an overwhelming majority; the *péquistes* won only seven of the 108 seats. Many Canadians breathed more easily, forgetting that René Lévesque had been supported by a quarter of the French-Canadian voters.

The failure of the Parti Québécois may have provoked even more extreme measures by the militant separatists in the Front de libération du Québec (FLQ). The FLQ's earlier terrorist activities—robberies and bombings that resulted in five deaths—suddenly escalated to direct confrontation with the governments of Canada and Quebec. On October 5, 1970, the FLQ kidnapped James Cross, the British trade commissioner in Montreal. In return for his release they demanded the release and safe passage to Cuba or Algeria of imprisoned members of the FLQ, $500,000 in gold, and the publication of an FLQ manifesto. The manifesto, which was read on Radio-Canada as the federal and provincial governments attempted to save the life of Mr. Cross, made it clear that the FLQ was not only a separatist organization, but also a revolutionary group whose heroes were Fidel Castro and Ché Guevara.

Five days after the Cross kidnapping, another FLQ cell kidnapped Pierre Laporte, a Quebec cabinet minister. Pressure mounted on the Ottawa and Quebec governments. The majority of Canadians, English and French, favoured a hard line; but radical Quebec nationalists and FLQ sympathizers attempted to stir up support for the FLQ. On October 15, faced with the danger of widespread civil disorder and warned that the police could no longer keep order, the Quebec government asked Prime Minister Trudeau to send the army into Quebec. A day later the Trudeau cabinet proclaimed the War Measures Act, which gave the police exceptional powers to seek out the kidnappers. The FLQ replied by strangling Pierre Laporte.

In the end James Cross was located and freed by his kidnappers in return for their safe passage to Cuba. The Laporte murderers were caught and brought to trial. By the spring of 1971 the immediate crisis was over. But the problems of separatism and economic and social reform remained. So, too,

A man for all seasons

did the scars in a nation that had to witness the suspension of civil liberties and the rule of law in order to deal with a small group of fanatics who preferred kidnapping and murder to the slow process of democracy.

The crisis of 1970 discredited the revolutionary ultranationalists. It also forced the Parti Québécois to emphasize even more that it favoured peaceful, gradual, and democratic changes in Quebec society. More importantly, their approach to the question of independence softened in both tone and substance. Lévesque began to speak of independence more in sadness than in anger; it might be painful, he admitted, but both societies would be happier in a union of the pocketbook instead of the heart. Finally, on the eve of the November 15, 1976, election, the party declared that its victory would not be regarded as a vote for independence. But if elected, it would hold a referendum on the issue during its first term of office.

The new *péquiste* strategy combined with increasing Liberal unpopularity to catapult the Parti Québécois into power. Opinion polls made it clear that the Québécois had voted more for good government than independence, and that a majority opposed separation. But the first momentous step had been taken.

"I don't think that's the answer, Sir." Senator Keith Davey, Liberal campaign organizer, suggests that a war with Lévesque may not be the best way for Trudeau to win the 1978 election.

Reprinted with permission—*The Toronto Star* Syndicate.

Once in office the Lévesque government began implementing its election promises, including a law making French the official language of Quebec, establishing it as the language of work, and compelling immigrants to Quebec to enroll their children in French rather than English schools. But while the work of government went on, so, too, did planning for the referendum. Since it was obvious that a majority did not support independence or even sovereignty-association, if association could not be guaranteed, the tactics to follow were clear. The government promised not to pursue independence unless the rest of Canada agreed to an economic association. Moreover, the whole idea of independence was played down.

The official referendum policy statement was called *Quebec–Canada: A New Deal,* and its subtitle spoke of "a new partnership between equals." The referendum itself did not ask the voter to support sovereignty-association, but to give the government a mandate to negotiate this "new deal." Finally, Premier Lévesque promised that whatever the outcome of the negotiations with the rest of Canada, the Quebec electorate would have the opportunity to approve or disapprove in another referendum.

The opponents of sovereignty-association underlined the economic cost of independence and the likely refusal of the rest of Canada to agree to economic association. They also argued that there was no contradiction in being a Quebec nationalist and a Canadian: "Choose Quebec and Canada," and, *"Mon Non est Québécois,"* proclaimed their campaign literature. However, they did not argue for the status quo, but for a radically restructured federal system. Prime Minister Trudeau entered the fray to proclaim his Canadianism and to promise his support for major constitutional changes through federal-provincial discussions. And all the other provincial premiers expressed their willingness to sit down and work with a greater sense of purpose and urgency than ever before.

On May 20, 1980, 59.5 percent of Quebeckers voted against René Lévesque's request for a mandate to negotiate sovereignty-association. While the anglophone vote was overwhelmingly No, a slight majority of francophone Quebeckers also voted No. To Prime Minister Trudeau the vote signaled the end of a "long period of uncertainty," and marked "a new beginning, a period of freedom and rebuilding. By voting for Canada, the people of Quebec recognize that their fellow Canadians are prepared to listen to them, to understand them and meet their legitimate aspirations." René Lévesque admitted that for the moment "the ball has been sent into the federalist camp. The Quebec people have clearly given them another chance . . . Let us accept, but not let go. It will come."

The fear that it would "come" was a major factor in the debate over the Canadian Constitution that really began in the 1960s and is not over yet. By the 1970s, other provinces had also become more interested in revising the Constitution, and we set out on the road that led to the Charter of Rights and Freedoms, Meech Lake, Charlottetown, and the next chapter in the history of separatism in Quebec.

9 The Road to a New Constitution—and Back

FOR TWENTY YEARS before the Quebec referendum on independence in 1980 the federal and provincial governments had been talking about reforming the Canadian Constitution. The first step, they agreed, was to devise a formula for amending the Constitution, and then to "patriate" the British North America Act, 1867, which was still an act of British Parliament. Before any agreement had been reached, however, the demands of Quebec, in particular, for more radical changes brought the distribution of legislative power and taxation—and even Quebec's special status in the federation—to the negotiating table. Pierre Trudeau changed the agenda dramatically when he became prime minister in 1968 and insisted that language guarantees and a Charter of Rights had to be included in any new constitution.

Pierre Trudeau had entered federal politics in 1965 to oppose the nationalists in Quebec and their demand for a "special status" with vastly greater powers. He believed that the Pearson government had been weak in allowing Quebec (and other provinces if they chose, but none did) to "opt out" of federal shared-cost programs. However, Trudeau firmly believed that bringing the Constitution home was a symbol of our nationhood, signifying the removal of the last remnant of our colonial origin. But he realized that unless there was an amending formula in place that would protect the provinces against any unilateral federal action, the provinces would not agree to patriation. Most significantly, he maintained that what was important was not which government had jurisdiction over what power, but how the rights and freedoms of the people could be protected against the laws and actions of all governments. Although Trudeau was brilliant and determined—some would add arrogant—he also knew that politics was the art of the possible, and that compromise was sometimes essential.

After three years of negotiations, in 1971, Trudeau and the provinces agreed to the Victoria Charter. The Charter guaranteed some political rights, such as the freedom of thought and expression, and some language rights. The federal government made some small concessions to Quebec in the field of social policy and gave the provinces a voice in the appointment of Supreme Court judges. The Constitution could be amended with the approval of the government of Canada, the governments of Ontario and Quebec, two of the Atlantic provinces, and two of the western provinces. This agreed, the Constitution would be patriated.

However, although all of the premiers agreed to these terms, Premier Robert Bourassa returned to Quebec to find nationalist critics, and even members of his own party, up in arms. The Victoria Charter, they insisted, was a disastrous defeat for everything Quebec had demanded since 1960. As a leading separatist put it, if Bourassa accepted the "Trudeau Charter" he would be "committing treason against the people of Quebec. If he accepts that, he accepts the death of Quebec." It was necessary to say "non," and after meeting with his cabinet and caucus, Bourassa did just that. The Victoria Charter was dead.

For the next five years the Constitution was put on the back burner as the country wrestled with the problems of recession, inflation, unemployment, and the enormous increases in oil prices imposed on the world by the major oil-

Cartoonist Chambers, like many anglophones, was not very sympathetic to Premier Bourassa's position on the Constitution.

producing countries in the Middle East and South America. The election of René Lévesque and the Parti Québécois in November 1976, with the promise of a referendum on independence, brought the time of waiting to an end. Moreover, the "oil shock," as it was called, had added an important new dynamic to the process of constitutional reform. As oil and gas prices soared, the Trudeau government had simultaneously frozen oil prices in Canada and increased taxes on the oil industry to get its share of the increased wealth flowing to the industry and the oil-producing western provinces, particularly Alberta. The West was outraged. Premier Lougheed of Alberta threatened to cut off oil and gas shipments to Eastern Canada, and many westerners echoed his comment: "Let the

The war in the West. Pierre Trudeau's "second coming" was a reference to his resignation after his defeat in 1979 and his change of mind when the government, led by Joe Clark, was defeated in the Commons and called an election in 1980.

Courtesy Vance Rodewalt.

---

eastern bastards freeze in the dark." Politically, westerners spoke sullenly of secession. Constitutionally, they were determined to increase their power at the expense of the federal government and within national institutions.

The debate over a new constitution raged for four years. Apart from generally wanting to increase their power at the expense of Ottawa, the provinces agreed on little else. Finally, with the defeat of the Quebec referendum, Prime Minister Trudeau declared that since no agreement was possible he would patriate the Constitution and include within it a Charter of Rights and Freedoms. The issue, he said, was clear: the provincial premiers simply wanted to increase their power while he wanted to increase the power of "the people." With the exception of Ontario and New Brunswick, the provinces were outraged and attempted to get the courts to declare that the federal government did not have the power to change the Constitution without their consent. When the Supreme Court of Canada decided that the federal government had the legal power, but that it was unconstitutional to make changes without a large measure of provincial consent—or, as Trudeau put it, it would be legal to proceed, but "not nice"—the bell rang for the last round. If the provinces wanted something better, they had to negotiate; if Trudeau wanted to be nice and secure provincial consent, he had to make compromises. The result was the new Constitution of 1982.

The centre-piece of the 1982 Constitution was the Canadian Charter of Rights and Freedoms, which will be discussed in chapter ten. The new Constitution also "recognized and affirmed" the "existing aboriginal and treaty rights" of the aboriginal people of Canada (Indian, Inuit, and Métis), although it was not clear exactly what that meant. All governments were committed to "promoting equal opportunities" for all Canadians, and the federal government, in particular, was now bound by the Constitution to make equalization payments. The Constitution also provided that it could be amended by Ottawa and two-thirds of the provinces who had among them fifty percent of the population, but any amendment that reduced provincial powers could only affect a province with its consent. The 1867 British North America Act (now patriated and renamed the Constitution Act, 1867) was also amended to expand and protect provincial powers over natural resources.

The 1982 constitutional settlement had one fatal political flaw: it was not accepted by the premier of Quebec. Indeed, a funny thing had happened on the way to the new

René Lévesque leaves the field as Trudeau and the nine provincial premiers celebrate the constitutional touchdown in 1982.

Constitution: a process that had begun largely as a response to the demands from Quebec had ended up with a settlement in which Quebec had less power than before. Quebec did not have a veto over amendments; it did not gain any additional legislative powers; and the Charter of Rights and Freedoms not only limited the rights of all governments, but also protected the language rights of anglophones in Quebec. While the rest of Canada celebrated on April 17, 1982, when Queen Elizabeth signed the new Constitution into law, angry mobs roamed the streets of Montreal and burned the Canadian flag.

As long as Pierre Trudeau, the antinationalist, and René Lévesque, the committed separatist, were in power there could be no chance of a constitutional settlement. But, in 1984, Trudeau resigned, and John Turner was chosen as the new leader of the Liberal party. During the election campaign that followed, the Conservative leader, Brian Mulroney, had promised a policy of "national reconciliation" to "bring Quebec back in." A year later, in Quebec's provincial election, the Parti Québécois was defeated by the federalist Liberals under Robert Bourassa. Taking Mulroney at his word, the Bourassa government soon set out the conditions that would enable them to accept a revised constitution. In 1987 at Meech Lake outside Ottawa, after months of negotiations, the prime minister and all provincial premiers agreed to constitutional amendments that satisfied Quebec.

By far the most controversial aspect of the agreement was the recognition of Quebec as a "distinct society," and that the provincial government had the responsibility to "preserve and promote" that distinct identity. At the same time the existence of a French- and English-speaking Canada was stated to be "a fundamental characteristic of Canada" that all governments were committed to "preserve." Other provisions permitted provinces to opt out of any new shared-cost programs and receive financial compensation from Ottawa if they introduced a comparable program; the provinces were to be given a voice in appointments to the Senate and the Supreme Court; and Quebec—and the other provinces if they wished—was given increased power over immigration. The Meech Lake Accord had to be adopted by Parliament and all the provincial legislatures by June 23, 1990.

On June 23, 1990, Meech Lake was dead. Technically it died when Elijah Harper, an aboriginal member of the Manitoba legislature, refused, on procedural grounds, to let a vote be taken, and when the new government in Newfoundland, under Premier Clyde Wells, failed to give its assent. But more generally it died because it had aroused intense opposition nationally.

While many Canadians argued that the Accord would fatally weaken the federal government, the most bitter criticism in English-speaking Canada was of the distinct society clause. Why should Quebec be regarded as distinct? If French Canadians were distinct, why not aboriginals, whose demands

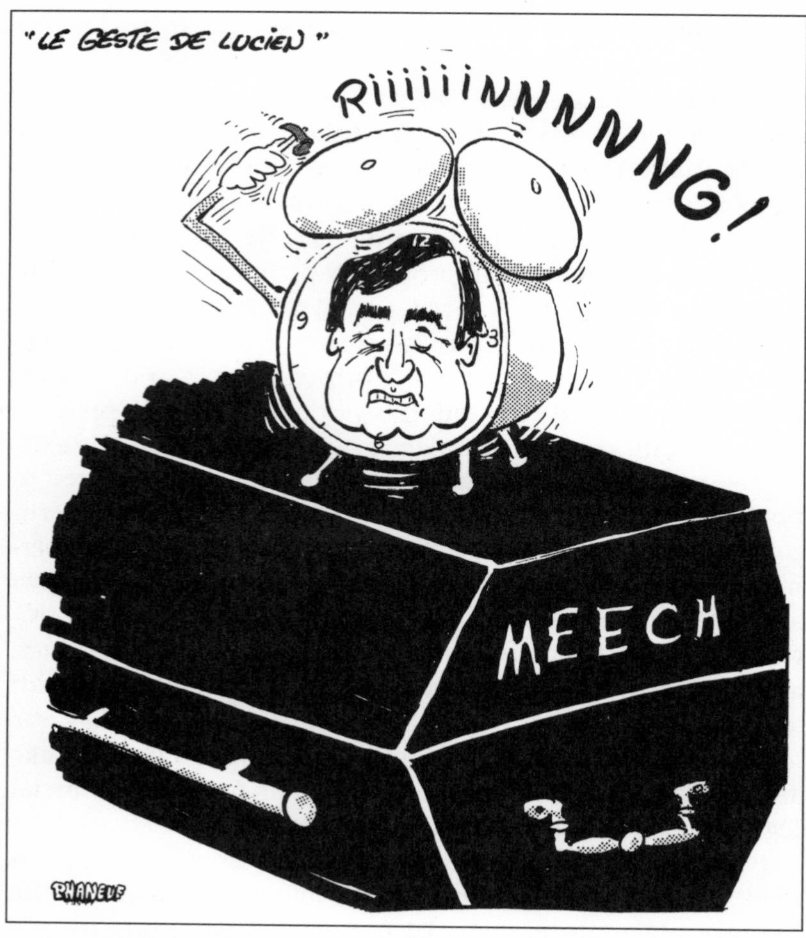

A month before the Meech Lake Accord was dead, Lucien Bouchard resigned from the Mulroney cabinet because he believed the government was going to weaken the agreement. An avowed separatist and sympathizer, if not supporter, of the Parti Québécois who had voted Yes in the 1980 referendum, Bouchard formed the Bloc Québécois soon after the death of the Meech Lake Accord on June 23, 1990.

Le Devoir, May 24, 1990.

---

for self-government had been ignored? Why should Quebec enjoy special status? Would the distinct society clause override the guarantees in the Charter, particularly English-language rights or women's rights in Quebec? Why should the rest of Canada be committed to maintaining bilingualism when the government of Quebec had ignored a Supreme Court decision stating that "French only" signs were a violation of the freedom of expression guaranteed by the Charter?

Pierre Trudeau entered the fray with a powerful emotional appeal to Canadians to reject Meech or "the Canada we know and love will be gone forever." In short, Meech Lake failed because it represented an elite consensus that carried little clout in a country fragmented by the clamour of language, culture, region, and rights.

Once again, it seemed, Quebec had been rejected. With Bourassa refusing to negotiate until the other provinces had firm proposals to discuss, and threatening to hold another referendum on Quebec's future in 1992, the process of constitutional reform began all over again. However, this was not to be a "Quebec round," but a "Canada round," with all provinces and all Canadians—tens of thousands of whom, from all walks of life, were given the opportunity to present their views—setting forth their demands. What emerged, in the Charlottetown Accord in the fall of 1992, were much more radical proposals for a new constitutional settlement. The ingredients from Meech Lake were still there, including distinct society, but in addition there were proposals for a Triple-E Senate, aboriginal self-government, a social charter, environmental protection, and the withdrawal of the federal government from the fields of housing, tourism, and even culture. No one got everything they wanted, but there was something for everyone, except the federal government—unless it was peace at any price.

Although the Accord had been accepted, albeit reluctantly, by every provincial government, 54.4 percent of the Canadian people voted No on October 26, 1992, after an emotional and bitter campaign. The vote was overwhelmingly No in Quebec and the four western provinces, and strongly Yes in three of the Atlantic provinces. Nova Scotia voted No by a narrow margin and Ontario said Yes by a few thousand votes. Political scientist Ronald Watts attempted to explain the result:

> *In the hurly-burly of the referendum debate the larger vision embodied in the Charlottetown consensus report was lost in the media and partisan preoccupations with specific provisions and with concerns about the extent to which each particular group had or had not achieved all its own specific aims. The result was an ensuing preoccupation with assessing losses under the agreement: Canadians seemed to become involved in a competition to see which province, region or group could lay claim to being the biggest losers as a result of the Charlottetown agreement. In the end, the political leaders found that in trying to accommodate every group they had drafted a document that because it required so many compromises made more enemies than friends. (*Canada: The State of the Federation 1993*, eds. R. W. Watts and D. M. Brown, 5)*

It was indeed a selfish or selfless calculation of profit and loss: too much or too little for the aboriginals, Quebec, the West, women, the left or the right, Ottawa or the provinces. Tragically, the defeat of the Accord did not blaze a trail into the future, but left Canada deep in a seemingly impenetrable constitutional jungle.

The federal election of October 1993 seemed to confirm the deep cultural, regional, and linguistic divisions, as well as the anger, within the country. After eight years of office, the Conservative party was annihilated, winning only two seats. Jean Chrétien's Liberals swept Ontario and the Maritimes and won seats in every province to win 178 in total and a comfortable majority. In Quebec, however, the separatist Bloc Québécois, formed only three years earlier, partly in response to the failure of Meech, won fifty-four out of seventy-five seats. In the West, the Reform Party, the six-year-old vehicle for the expression of western discontent and anti-Quebec

How the *Toronto Star* editorial cartoonist pictured the defeat of the Charlottetown Accord. It was not only Brian Mulroney who was slugged, but all the provincial premiers, as well.

Reprinted with permission—*The Toronto Star* Syndicate.

sentiments, swept British Columbia and Alberta and ran second in Saskatchewan, Manitoba, and even Ontario. When the new Parliament opened in January 1994 there were, in effect, two opposition parties to the Liberal government: Lucien Bouchard's Bloc Québécois, who, ironically, wanted out of Canada; and Preston Manning's Reform party, who were not prepared to make any concessions to keep Quebec in. For the moment there was little anyone could do until Quebec went to the polls later in 1994. But if the votes against the Charlottetown Accord and for the Bloc were any indication, the Québécois were likely to return the separatists to power with a mandate to negotiate some form of independence. And academic and political pundits began to write learned articles and hold learned conferences to discuss the future of that new country, ROC, or CWOQ—the Rest of Canada, or Canada Without Quebec.

10 The Charter of Rights and Freedoms

The Charter of Rights and Freedoms will probably be remembered as Pierre Trudeau's most lasting—perhaps his only lasting—gift to the Canadian people. Whether you realize it or not, if you have ever been stopped in a spot-check, arrested, had drugs in your possession, gambled illegally, rented a movie from an adult video store, thought of having an abortion, or voted in the last three federal elections, the Charter has influenced your life. If you are a university professor, a dentist, a firefighter in Alberta, a nurse in the Northwest Territories, a doctor in British Columbia, an immigrant applying for refugee status, or a Sunday shopper, you have not escaped the legacy left by Pierre Elliott Trudeau.

Trudeau grew up in the province of Quebec when it was governed by Maurice Duplessis, a man never known for his respect for civil liberties or the pure workings of a democracy. Long before he entered politics, as a young lawyer, Trudeau had advocated a declaration of human rights, and the subject of one of his first speeches after becoming minister of justice in 1967 was "A Constitutional Declaration of Rights." What was urgently needed, he argued, was a charter of rights, broad in scope and including language rights, that would be so deeply entrenched in the Constitution that the rights could not be violated by the provincial or federal governments. As prime minister he pursued the cause with that stubborn determination that marked his career. For better or for worse, he gave us the Charter, which for him had become much more than an assertion of the rights of the individual against the state; the Charter was to serve as a unifying force, a basis of common Canadianism.

Opposition to the idea of an entrenched Charter of Rights and Freedoms was widespread and intense. It came from the left and the right, from those who either said it went too far or not far enough. The most vocal opposition came from those responsible for law enforcement, who warned that too strict an adherence to legal rights would hamper their work and serve only to protect the guilty. The most principled opposition came from those who argued that a charter embodying rights and freedoms that could not be touched by governments was a rejection of democracy. Since the courts would determine whether laws violated the Charter, an unelected judiciary would replace Parliament at the apex of the Canadian political system. It was not difficult to make the point that elected governments were far more likely to reflect Canadian values than nine men and women on the Supreme Court of Canada whose decisions would be final and conclusive. Nor was it difficult to argue that by education, experience, and income lawyers and judges were wealthy members of the establishment whose decisions would reflect their social and economic bias.

Application of Charter

33. (1) Parliament or the legislature of a province may expressly declare in an Act of Parliament or of the legislature, as the case may be, that the Act or a provision thereof shall operate notwithstanding a provision included in section 2 or sections 7 to 15 of this Charter.

To secure provincial consent Trudeau finally had to make one important concession. Section 33 of the Charter provided that the federal or provincial governments could pass

"Pss-ss-st! . . . . I know a place where we can speak English. . . ."

By the late 1970s language had become the most emotional issue in Canada. While Trudeau was attempting to move the country towards greater bilingualism, Lévesque's famous Bill 101 had declared French the only official language in Quebec, while also forbidding immigrants to attend English-language schools and ordering all stores and businesses to have all their signs and advertisements in French only. Cartoonist Delatri makes his position clear.

The Supreme Court declared much of the legislation unconstitutional, and there was an enormous outcry in English Canada when the Bourassa government used the notwithstanding clause in the Charter when the Supreme Court threw out the sign law as violating the right to freedom of expression.

---

laws that violated the freedoms and legal rights of the Charter provided they openly admitted that they were doing so. While this provision weakened the Charter it also protected parliamentary supremacy. However, Trudeau and others believed that few governments would so openly defy the Charter unless they knew the voters would approve. So far, at least, they have been right.

The Charter presented the courts an empty chalkboard on which the judges could write a new definition of individual rights and determine new boundaries between the individual and the state. How the courts—particularly the Supreme Court of Canada—viewed their role would determine whether the Charter would change Canadian society or leave it much as it was. Some feared and others hoped that the courts would be very active and would seize the opportunity to give a very expansive scope to rights and freedoms, striking down laws or prohibiting actions by the police that infringed upon those rights. Others hoped or feared that the judiciary would be very restrained and defer whenever possible to the will of the legislature. Would their decisions reflect the conservative biases of the social class to which most judges belonged? Would they dare venture into unknown ethical and philosophical territory and give concrete meaning to such phrases as the "right to life," and "freedom of conscience"? After ten years of Charter decisions the answer to all questions is clear: sometimes Yes and sometimes No.

There was, at the beginning, some misunderstanding about the Charter. Only laws or acts of governments—federal, provincial, and municipal—and their agents, such as the police, could trigger a Charter appeal. Protection of an individual's rights against private discrimination, for example, remained with provincial human rights commissions. Moreover, the rights and freedoms guaranteed in the Charter are not absolute. Individual rights must be balanced against the rights and interests of society as a whole. That principle was clearly stated in Section 1 of the Charter, the "reasonable limits" clause.

This is not an introductory text in constitutional law, but it is important for Canadians to understand the process of Charter litigation. Normally, appeals to the Charter will be made by someone who is accused of a crime and, in defence, will argue that the law under which they are charged—for example, a law apparently limiting their freedom of expres-

CANADIAN CHARTER OF RIGHTS AND FREEDOMS

Whereas Canada is founded upon principles that recognize the supremacy of God and the rule of law:

Guarantee of Rights and Freedoms

1. The Canadian Charter of Rights and Freedoms guarantees the rights and freedoms set out in it subject only to such reasonable limits prescribed by law as can be demonstrably justified in a free and democratic society.

Fundamental Freedoms

2. Everyone has the following fundamental freedoms:
   (a) freedom of conscience and religion;
   (b) freedom of thought, belief, opinion and expression, including freedom of the press and other media of communication;
   (c) freedom of peaceful assembly; and
   (d) freedom of association.

Legal Rights

7. Everyone has the right to life, liberty and security of the person and the right not to be deprived thereof except in accordance with the principles of fundamental justice.
8. Everyone has the right to be secure against unreasonable search or seizure.
9. Everyone has the right not to be arbitrarily detained or imprisoned.
10. Everyone has the right on arrest or detention
    (a) to be informed promptly of the reasons therefor;
    (b) to retain and instruct counsel without delay and to be informed of that right; and
    (c) to have the validity of the detention determined by way of habeas corpus and to be released if the detention is now lawful.
11. Any person charged with an offence has the right
    (a) to be informed without unreasonable delay of the specific offence;
    (b) to be tried within a reasonable time; . . .
    (c) to be presumed innocent until proven guilty according to law in a fair and public hearing by an independent and impartial tribunal; . . .
12. Everyone has the right not to be subjected to any cruel and unusual treatment or punishment.

Equality Rights

15. (1) Every individual is equal before and under the law and has the right to the equal protection and equal benefit of the law without discrimination and, in particular, without discrimination based on race, national or ethnic origin, colour, religion, sex, age or mental or physical disability. . . .

sion—in itself violates the rights or freedoms guaranteed in the Charter. Or that in arresting this individual, the police violated his or her right to legal counsel. But first the Court must determine what those rights are. How broad is the right to freedom of expression? Exactly what does the right to counsel mean, and when does it become operative? If the Court decides there has been a violation, the judges proceed to the second step of the inquiry.

In the case of a law that violates the Charter, the Court must then look at Section 1. Here the burden is on the government passing the law to prove that it is a "reasonable limit" that can be "justified in a free and democratic society." In other words, it represents a reasonable balance between the interests of society as a whole and the absolute rights of the individual. If that cannot be demonstrated to the satisfaction of the Court, the law is thrown out because Section 52 of the 1982 Constitution states: "The Constitution of Canada [of which the Charter is a part] is the supreme law of Canada, and any law that is inconsistent with the provisions of the Constitution is, to the extent of the inconsistency, of no force or effect."

In the case of a police action, if the Court decides that the right to counsel was violated and a confession or evidence was secured, the judges move to Section 24(2) of the Charter. Section 24(2) states that if "a court concludes that evidence was obtained in a manner that infringed or denied any rights or freedoms guaranteed by this Charter, the evidence shall be excluded if it is established that, having regard to all the circumstances, the admission of it in the proceedings would bring the administration of justice into disrepute." In other words, if the police denied an accused the right to counsel—that is, consulting a lawyer—then secured a confession, the court could decide that the use of that confession at trial would make the judicial system seem unfair.

It should be apparent that from beginning to end there is enormous room for judicial discretion when an appeal is made to the Charter. Law, and certainly Charter law, is not a mathematical formula that can be applied to any given case, but is often a question of individual judgement. Does the freedom of expression include pornography? What is a "reasonable limit"? Would the acquittal of an obviously guilty person because of some technical infringement regarding their conviction or their right to counsel, no matter what the violation, not be more likely to bring the administration of justice into disrepute? There are no hard and fast answers, and the judges on the Supreme Court of Canada have differed among themselves on these issues, as would ordinary Canadians not trained in the law. Nevertheless, since its institution, there have been thousands and thousands of Charter cases in the courts across the country, and hundreds have reached the Supreme Court. (Lawyers, feasting on their fees, win or lose, should be grateful to Pierre Trudeau.) A few brief outlines of some cases decided by the Supreme Court, here, will help illustrate the nature of Charter litigation.

Presumption of Innocence: Section 11(d), *R. v. Oakes**

David Oakes was found in possession of eight ounces of hashish oil. Section 8 of the federal Narcotics Control Act stated that an accused found guilty of possession of narcotics would also be found guilty of trafficking unless he or she could prove otherwise. In defence, Oakes's lawyers argued that Section 8 violated 11(d) of the Charter, because it placed the burden of proof of innocence for the charge of trafficking on the accused, rather than the burden of proving guilt on the prosecution. The Supreme Court unanimously decided that the "reverse onus" provision of the Narcotics Control Act that attached trafficking to possession could not be justified under Section 1, on the grounds that it was too broad and could lead to the imprisonment of people who had only one joint for their own use.

*R. stands for *Regina*, or the Queen, and indicates the criminal law case is really the government versus Oakes.

Freedom of Expression: Section 2(b), *R. v. Butler*

Donald Victor Butler owned a "hard core" video shop. He was charged with selling obscene material, contrary to the provisions of the Criminal Code, which defined as obscene "any publication a dominant characteristic of which is the undue exploitation of sex, or of sex and any one or more of the following subjects, namely, crime, horror, cruelty and violence." A unanimous Supreme Court found that Section 163 violated the right of freedom of expression, but concluded it was a justifiable limitation under Section 1 in the interests of society as a whole.

Freedom of Expression: Section 2(b), *R. v. Keegstra*

James Keegstra, an Alberta high school teacher, was charged under Section 319 of the Criminal Code with unlawfully promoting hatred against an identifiable group by communicating anti-Semitic statements to his students, and expecting them to reproduce his views on their exams or suffer poor marks. The code also provided a defence if the accused proved that the statements were true. In defence, Keegstra argued that Section 319 of the code violated both 2(b) and 11(d) of the Charter. The Court unanimously agreed that both sections were infringed. However, four members of the Court decided that the violations were justifiable under Section 1. Three judges concluded that neither violation was justified under Section 1, on the grounds that there was no evidence that the criminalization of hate propaganda achieved the objective of stopping it, and that the publicity given to such cases might have the opposite effect, which would not be in the best interests of society. In short, the cost of using Section 1 outweighed the benefits.

Freedom of Expression: Section 2(b), *R. v. Zundel*

Ernst Zundel had published a pamphlet about the Holocaust entitled "Did Six Million Jews Really Die?" He was charged under Section 181 of the Criminal Code, which states that "Everyone who wilfully publishes a statement, tale or news that he knows is false and that causes or is likely to cause injury or mischief to a public interest is guilty of an indictable offence . . ." The Court was unanimous in finding that Section 181 of the code violated Section 2(b) of the Charter, and that even outright lies were covered by freedom of expression. Four members decided that Section 181 was not justified under Section 1 of the Charter, three believed that it was.

Freedom of Association: Section 2(d), Alberta Compulsory Arbitration Act

The government of Alberta prohibited strikes by police, firefighters, and hospital workers. Differences over wages would have to be settled by compulsory arbitration. The workers affected argued that the prohibition against striking violated their right to freedom of association because the strike weapon was an essential purpose of the association or trade union. In a four-to-two decision, the Supreme Court decided that the right to strike was not protected by the Charter. The minority argued, in effect, that to take away the right to strike from a union was like sending an army into battle without weapons. This decision, and several others like it, has been denounced by some critics who say that it confirms the fear of class bias among the judiciary.

Right to Counsel: Section 10(b), *R. v. Clarkson*

Mrs. Clarkson was intoxicated on the night her husband was shot to death. She was arrested and informed of her right to counsel. Although her sister warned her not to answer questions without getting a lawyer, Mrs. Clarkson said it did not matter, confessed to the murder, and was later convicted of murder on the basis of her confession. On appeal, her lawyers claimed that she was too drunk to understand the importance of remaining silent and retaining counsel. The Supreme Court agreed. Finding a violation, the Court turned to Section 24 of the Charter and concluded that the use of her confession at the trial had brought the administration of justice into disrepute and, therefore, could not be used. The Supreme Court acquitted Clarkson and unless other evidence could be secured for a new trial she would be free.

Right to Life, Liberty, and Security of the Person:

Section 7, *R. v. Morgentaler*

The case of Dr. Henry Morgentaler is the most celebrated, and one of the most complicated, in Charter history. The Criminal Code made it a crime to secure an abortion unless it was done by a qualified doctor, in a hospital, with the approval of a hospital committee, and then only if the life or health of the woman was in danger. Dr. Morgentaler believed that every woman had the right to a safe and legal abortion and started clinics to provide abortions on demand. He was frequently arrested, convicted, and jailed. Ultimately he appealed to the Supreme Court, where he claimed the required procedure violated the woman's right not to be deprived of "life, liberty, and the security of the person . . . except in accordance with principles of fundamental justice."

The questions before the Court were easy to frame, if difficult to answer. Did "security of the person" mean women had the right to terminate a pregnancy? Did a fetus enjoy the "right to life"? Was the procedure required to obtain a legal abortion in accordance with the "principles of fundamental justice"? The Court was very divided. Four judges concluded that the complicated procedure and the refusal of some doctors and some hospitals to perform abortions at all was unfair to some women and, therefore, violated the principles of fundamental justice. They did not say whether the woman had the "right" to an abortion, although it would seem to have been implied. Two judges denied categorically that any right to an abortion could be found anywhere in the language of Section 7, and argued that if Parliament had wanted to make abortion a right in the Charter, the language would have been explicit. Parliament had decided what procedure must be followed to secure an abortion, and it was not for the Court to second-guess or change Parliament's decision.

Only one judge, Bertha Wilson, directly confronted the real issue. She declared that a woman had the right to an abortion, and that the legislation clearly violated both freedom of conscience and Section 7. Even she, however, admitted that at some point in the later stages of pregnancy the state had the right to protect the fetus. In the end a majority of five to two decided that the section of the Criminal Code was invalid. Morgentaler was free to operate his clinics; Canada was without any abortion legislation, and still is because no middle ground has been found between those who support and those who oppose a woman's right to abortion that seems politically acceptable.

Impaired Driving: Sections 9 and 10(b)

The cases that strike closest to home for many people involve impaired driving, and inventive lawyers have sought refuge for their clients in many sections of the Charter, Sections 9 and 10(b), in particular. After a large number of Charter decisions the case law in this area now seems fairly clear: The police may stop you for whatever reason, or for no reason, and although the detention may be arbitrary and in violation of Section 9, the legislation authorizing the police to patrol the highways has been upheld as a justifiable limit to maintain safety (*Therens, Hufsky, Thomsen, Ladouceur*). If asked to breathe into a roadside breathalyser, "forthwith," as the law states, you must comply or face criminal charges. The Court has held that your right to counsel when detained (Section 10[b]) does not apply to a roadside test. The results of that test cannot be used as evidence against you, but, if the test is positive, under the law you may be taken to the police station, where an admissible test may be administered. At that point you must be informed without delay of your right to secure counsel, or your Section 10(b) right will have been violated (*Therens*,

In 1982 Prime Minister Trudeau appointed Bertha Wilson to the Supreme Court of Canada—the first woman to be given such an appointment. The event inspired Andy Donato's editorial cartoon, reprinted here, with Chief Justice Bora Laskin talking to members of the Court. As a member of the Supreme Court, Justice Wilson always gave a broad scope to the rights and freedoms in the Charter, and was extremely reluctant to conclude that any limit by the government was permissible under Section 1, or that any evidence should be included at a trial that was secured in violation, however trivial, of a Charter right.

Tremblay), and the evidence from the test may be excluded. However, if you are not diligent in the attempt to find a lawyer, in the hope that the alcohol level in your blood will fall below the impaired level, you may be asked to take the test and the evidence could be included at trial despite the violation (*Tremblay*). In almost every case, the Court has decided that legislation to curb drinking and driving is a slight and demonstrably justifiable limitation on legal rights.

The decisions of the Supreme Court of Canada are binding on all lower courts across Canada. Those decisions place the same limitations on the powers of all governments, and give all Canadians the same rights and freedoms. In that sense the Charter is a unifying force.

On the other hand, the Charter is also a divisive force. Does the right to equality (Section 15) mean that any group or person disadvantaged on the grounds of race, ethnicity, or gender has the right to have that inequality erased, even at the expense of other groups or individuals? Did the instruction to the courts to interpret the Charter "in a manner consistent with the preservation and enhancement of the multicultural heritage of Canada" give some special rights to racial, ethnic, or linguistic minorities? And if some rights are guaranteed, why not others? If yours, why not mine?

The debate over rights launched by the Charter changed the nature of Canadian politics. Most issues of public policy can be decided through compromise and consensus, and remain relatively flexible. But rights, once asserted, become absolutes; it is hard to bargain over them. When it comes to issues such as abortion, rights can be a source of division and conflict that serve to fragment society, and in so doing paralyse politicians whose aim it is to win friends while not making enemies. However, once a system of establishing and protecting rights and freedoms of all individuals living in a democracy is put in place there is no turning back. No one ever said it would be easy.

11 The World Beyond

IT WAS A PROUD MOMENT for Canada in 1957 when Lester Pearson, the secretary of state for External Affairs, received the Nobel Peace Prize. Pearson's fertile mind, quiet diplomacy, and unflinching determination helped to prevent a crisis in the Middle East from becoming another world war. The prize proved that Canada, not one of the great world powers, could play an important role in international affairs. It suggested that because Canada was not a great power it would be accepted as the "honest broker" or the "helpful fixer" among nations.

Compared to the European powers or the United States, Canada has had relatively few years of experience in foreign affairs. Before World War I, Canada had no foreign policy, for, although it was self-governing in all internal matters, the British government controlled the foreign policy of the whole empire. When Britain went to war in 1914 Canada was automatically at war.

However, it was Canada that determined how much it would contribute to the Allied war effort. For a nation of eight million the Canadian contribution was impressive. Over 600,000 men and women were in uniform; 60,000 failed to return from the battlefield in Europe, and tens of thousands of others were permanently disabled. Canadian troops were regarded as among the best—if not *the* best—in the Allied army. As the British prime minister wrote of the capture of Vimy Ridge by the Canadians in 1917, "the

Canadians in France, 1916.

Canadians played a part of such distinction that henceforth they were marked out as storm troops; for the remainder of the war they were brought along to head one assault after another." The heroism at the front gave an enormous stimulus to Canadian pride and nationalism. If men went to the front as British subjects, they returned as Canadians. If Canada went to war as a colony, it emerged as a nation, free to conduct its own foreign policy and to take its own place on the world stage as a member of the League of Nations.

Despite this recognition, Canada played a limited role in international affairs in the 1920s and the 1930s. Some Canadians believed that Canada should stand "Ready, aye Ready" behind Britain, but most did not. The war had bitterly divided English and French Canadians over the question of compulsory military service and, to some extent, whether Canada should be involved in Britain's wars at all. Restoring and preserving national unity was one of the major tasks facing the government after the war. Staying out of the affairs of Europe and avoiding the risk of being engulfed in another war seemed a wise policy.

But a policy of "isolation" meant that Canada had to firmly establish its independence from Britain and limit its commitments to the League of Nations. William Lyon Mackenzie King, the prime minister throughout the 1920s and again from 1935 to 1948, was determined to do both. When the British proposed at the Imperial Conference of 1923 that despite their new status all the Dominions in the Empire should agree to a common foreign policy, necessarily directed by them, King was adamantly opposed. "The obstacle has been Mackenzie King," growled the British foreign minister, "who is both obstinate, tiresome and stupid." King's insistence that Canada would follow its own policy and would not be bound by any British commitments carried the day. "You ought to be satisfied," commented General Smuts of South Africa, "Canada has had her way in everything." Three years later at the Imperial Conference of 1926, Britain and the Dominions redefined their relations, and in so doing changed the British Empire into the Commonwealth of Nations:

> *They are autonomous Dominions within the British Empire, equal in status, in no way subordinate one to another in any aspect of their domestic or external affairs, though united by a common allegiance to the Crown and freely associated as members of the British Commonwealth of Nations.*

The necessary legal changes to confirm Canada's independence were made in the Statute of Westminster in 1931.

Mackenzie King was also determined to limit Canada's commitments to the League of Nations, particularly the obligations under Article X to fight, if necessary, to protect other countries in the League from aggression. The United States had not joined for that reason, and many Canadians believed the Americans had made the right decision. Rather than leave the League, however, King was determined to weaken Article X. As the Canadian delegate to the League explained in 1924, "in this association of Mutual Insurance against fire, the risks assumed by the different states are not equal. We live in a fireproof house far from inflammable materials." In the end Canada succeeded in having a resolution passed whereby the League agreed to take into account a country's geographical position and national interest before asking for military support. That effectively cut Canadian commitments beyond the Americas. King's policy of isolation perhaps reflected Canadian opinion, but it was not long before Hitler ended the myth of the "fireproof house."

Canada played little part in the events leading up to World War II. Following the German invasion of Poland, Britain declared war against Germany on September 3, 1939, and Canada declared war one week later. In contrast to 1914, Canada declared war as an independent state. And when Japanese bombs rained down on Pearl Harbor on December 7, 1941, the Canadian government immediately declared war on the island empire. Before the war ended in 1945, over 700,000 Canadians had seen active service, and 40,000 had lost their lives in Europe, Africa, and Asia. Canadian farms provided the food needed by the Allied forces, and Canadian factories produced 400 ships, 6,500 tanks, and 16,000 aircraft. The country had also played the major role of training the aircrews for the Commonwealth air forces. Under the Commonwealth Air Training Plan, 70,000 Canadians and 60,000 men from Britain, Australia, and New Zealand received their wings at Canadian air bases.

World War II radically changed the way Canadians viewed their role in world affairs. The isolationism of the interwar period was dead. So, too, was the distrust of collective security through international organizations that had helped to destroy the League. Canada was now determined to participate fully in world affairs and was finally convinced that collective security was the way to stop aggression in the future.

In the early months of World War II, critics accused the King government of doing little to mobilize the human and industrial resources of the country. King appealed to the country in 1940 and won a sweeping victory. This cartoon was published in opposition advertising.

Canada played its first major role at the San Francisco Conference that created the United Nations in 1945. Canadian diplomats did not claim great power status, but argued forcefully and successfully that Canada was not a small but a middle power whose voice must be heard. The country became and remains one of the most determined and consistent supporters of the United Nations, not only in collective security, but in the vast array of humanitarian, economic, and social activities the UN agencies perform.

Despite its small size, by the 1980s Canada was the fourth largest financial contributor to the UN. Canada has been an influential member of the General Assembly and has served with distinction on the Security Council. The most visible and dramatic contribution to the UN, however, has been the

Canadian role in "peacekeeping," a term used to describe a wide range of actions from all-out war to supervising uneasy truces or getting food to the starving. From Kashmir and Palestine in 1948 to Bosnia and Rwanda in 1994, Canadians have been involved in every major UN peacekeeping operation and have been described as "peacekeepers to the world."

The first critical test of the United Nations came in 1950 when Russian-controlled North Korea launched an invasion to "liberate" South Korea. In the West this was not seen as an isolated act in the Pacific, but, with the Soviet Union already taking effective control of all of Eastern Europe, as another case of Communist expansion. Would the West back down as it had in Munich in 1938, when Hitler had absorbed Czechoslovakia? Would collective security even work?

The answers were not long in coming. Led by the United States, the UN Security Council immediately issued a call to arms and fifty-three members declared their support. Initially, Canada sent three destroyers and a squadron of transport aircraft, but hesitated to commit to ground troops. A month later, with the war going badly and the Americans pressing for assistance, Canada sent a brigade of 5,000 men to fight alongside the Brits, Aussies, Indians, and New Zealanders, as part of a Commonwealth division. Some Canadian pilots also served with the American air force in the world's first air battles between jets. The UN forces fought not only the North Koreans with Soviet armaments, but also a massive Red Chinese army sent by Mao Zedong. Neither side could defeat the other, and when a truce was signed in 1953 the armies were back to where they began. It was not a great military victory. But at a cost of 370,000 dead, including 312 Canadians, and 1,200 Canadian wounded, the UN and the Western World had demonstrated that they would not back down in the face of aggression.

The next great test came in 1956 when Israel attacked Egypt and was joined by Britain and France, who opposed Egypt's plans to nationalize the strategic Suez Canal. As the

A Canadian soldier befriends some Korean children behind the lines during a lull in the fighting.

world teetered on the edge of a major war, Lester Pearson urged the United Nations to place a peacekeeping force in the battle zone to separate the combatants, and Canadian diplomats lobbied in the capitals of the world to have the plan accepted. Canada supplied the commander and a sixth of the peacekeeping force.

The Canadian role was not the easiest one to play. The Canadian government had reacted to the British attack "like finding a beloved uncle arrested for rape," commented a British magazine, but many Canadians believed that Canada should have supported Britain and Israel in their war against the Egyptian dictator. Nevertheless, the government had acted wisely, and Pearson deserved his Nobel Prize.

After Suez it seemed that every UN peacekeeping operation had to have a Canadian contingent. By the 1990s Canadians had served or were serving in Africa, the Middle East, Latin America, Vietnam, Laos and Cambodia, Afghanistan and Pakistan, the islands of New Guinea in the Pacific and Cyprus in the Mediterranean. Almost 85,000 Canadians had served on UN and other peacekeeping missions. When the 1988 Nobel Peace Prize was awarded to UN peacekeepers, Canadians rightly believed that much of the prize was theirs.

Peacekeeping in the 1970s and 1980s had not captured the attention of the media, but that changed dramatically in the 1990s. Operation Desert Storm in 1991 seemed almost like a TV movie, when the UN marshaled a U.S.-led force of 750,000 men and women from thirty-seven countries to liberate Kuwait from Saddam Hussein, the tyrannical leader of Iraq. Canada contributed a small naval and air contingent and, as usual, sent a peacekeeping force after the war to patrol the Iraq-Kuwait border.

Then came the tragedy in Somalia when a civil war made it impossible for relief agencies to get food to the hundreds of thousands of starving Somalis. The UN began an airlift in the fall of 1992 and then found it necessary to send in ground troops to secure the airports and protect the relief convoys from the armies of rival warlords. Again Canadians were on the ground and in the air, but it was soon clear that there could no be no long-term solution to the problem in Somalia until political stability and peace were restored in the country.

That lesson was reinforced by the experience in Bosnia when the republic of Yugoslavia disintegrated into fragments in 1991. UN peacekeepers, including a large Canadian contingent, were sent to monitor an uneasy truce between Serbia and Croatia in 1992, but in the spring civil war broke out in Bosnia, between Serbs, Croats, and Bosnian Muslims. When thousands of helpless civilians were killed as the Serbs began their campaign of "ethnic cleansing," in what appeared to be a campaign to exterminate the Bosnian Muslims, the UN sent in Canadian and other peacekeepers to keep the airports and roads open so that humanitarian supplies could get through. But the peacekeepers were really the prisoners of the large armies surrounding them, and routinely were shot at and roughed up without the capacity to fight back. With no prospect of peace in a war in which 200,000 were dead or missing—the greatest carnage since World War II—Canada and other countries wondered whether they should not end a policy better described as "armed humanitarianism" than peacekeeping.

In February 1994, the guns in the hills surrounding the beleaguered Bosnian city of Sarajevo fell silent when the UN and NATO threatened air strikes against Serbian gun emplacements, despite the threat of retaliation against the peacekeepers. But few believed that peace would come until the future of Bosnia was settled by the warring factions. Meanwhile, 2,000 Canadians—eight of whose comrades had died—wearing the blue beret of the UN in Bosnia and along the Serb-Croatian border, wondered whether they would get home or become the victims of an even larger conflict. They may have taken some comfort in an editorial in the *Globe and Mail* (6 January 1994) that expressed the views of many Canadians:

> *Are the UN troops ending the war? No. Are they making the combat any less savage? Perhaps not. Are they saving lives? Yes, thousands and thousands of them. In a brutal conflict that has made the whole world feel helpless, that at least is something.*

However valuable the UN has been as a peacekeeping and humanitarian body, it became clear soon after 1945 that it would not be able to resolve conflicts between the two great powers, the United States and the former Soviet Union. By 1946 the Cold War had begun and Winston Churchill warned of the "iron curtain" that was descending in Eastern Europe. In 1947, as one Eastern European state after another fell under Soviet control, two Canadian diplomats, Lester Pearson and Escott Reid, began to float the idea of a North Atlantic military alliance. And in the fall, Louis St. Laurent, then secretary of state for External Affairs in Canada, suggested at the UN that if it could not take action in a certain situation, the western democracies might seek "greater safety in an association of democratic and peace-loving states willing to accept more specific obligations in return for a greater measure of national security." The communist coup in Czechoslovakia in 1948 removed any lingering doubts in Canada and abroad about setting up such a mechanism, and in 1949 the North Atlantic Treaty Organization (NATO) was formed. For both Canada and the United States the creation of NATO marked the end of isolation, the end of the myth of the "fireproof house." Two years later units of the Canadian Army and Air Force were stationed in Germany. Canadians remained in Europe until 1993 after the momentous changes in the Soviet Union heralded the end of the Cold War.

The Cold War also served to cement the military alliance of Canada and the United States, which had begun in 1940 during World War II, when President Roosevelt assured Canadians that the United States, although neutral, would come to their aid if they were attacked. The two countries created the Permanent Joint Board of Defence. With North America vulnerable to attack by Soviet bombers—and later missiles—across the Arctic, the United States and Canada cooperated in building three lines of radar stations in Northern Canada after the war. Finally in 1958 they signed the North American Air Defence Agreement (NORAD, now called the North American Aerospace Defence Command), which integrated the defence of the continent against a Soviet air attack.

This close association between Canada and the United States has not always been comfortable. President Kennedy was outraged when Prime Minister Diefenbaker refused to put Canadian forces on "alert" during the Cuban missile crisis in 1962. President Johnson literally roughed up Prime Minister Pearson when he dared to criticize American policy in Vietnam in 1965. And the Americans were initially less than pleased when Pierre Trudeau decided to recognize Communist China in 1970. Canadians have often felt that the giant was too quick

"Now, as for press statements on our talks—here's yours."

Trudeau and President Richard Nixon: A not uncommon view of the relations between Canada and the superpower, despite the rhetoric of "hands across the border."

Reprinted with permission—*The Toronto Star* Syndicate.

---

in using the big stick, as it had in Vietnam and would again in Desert Storm, Somalia and, on occasion, had suggested it might be wielded in Bosnia. Although Canada approved of many of the objectives of American foreign policy, some maintained that Washington was too often driven by its capitalist ideology and economic interests. Was it likely, with the end of the Communist threat, that the alliance would unravel? Or did economic integration with free trade make a truly independent foreign policy improbable?

Although Canada's primary international contacts were within the UN and the North American alliance, it also developed a close association with nonwestern nations. Just as Canada had played a leading role in the creation of the British Commonwealth of Nations in the 1920s, so, too, did it play a critical role in the creation of the Commonwealth of Nations after 1945. When India became independent in 1947 and decided to become a republic that did not recognize the British monarch as the head of state, the question arose as to whether the Commonwealth should be expanded to admit the Asian giant. Canada believed that it should, and urged the British to forget the bitterness of the struggle for independence and brush aside the legal formalities. India chose to remain within the new, non-British Commonwealth, and where India led other newly independent nations in Africa and Asia followed to create one of the world's few multiracial organizations. Reflecting its own bicultural makeup, Canada also became a member of International Francophonie, a loose association of French-speaking countries, most of which were once part of the French colonial empire.

The Commonwealth and la Francophonie gave Canada a door to the Third World. With no imperial past and no imperial ambitions, Canada has earned a special position of trust in the nonwhite world. Canadian leaders can talk freely with Indians, as Pearson did during the Suez crisis, Ghanians, and Tanzanians. This trust was strengthened by Canada's opposition to racial discrimination. The decision to press South Africa to leave the Commonwealth because of its discriminatory policies was partly the result of Canadian action.

But above all, the developing nations of the Third World, particularly the Commonwealth countries, were grateful to Canada for the billions of dollars of Canadian foreign aid they received. As early as 1950 Canada helped to establish the Colombo Plan to provide economic assistance to the new Commonwealth countries, which found that economic development was far more difficult to achieve than political independence. By 1970 Canada was spending over a billion dollars a year. Twenty years later, despite serious financial problems at home, Canada was the world's seventh largest donor of foreign aid as a percentage of Gross Domestic Product, and ranked second among the G7 nations. From the teeming cities of India to the Sahara desert, from the forests of Indonesia to the rangelands of Kenya, the Canadian presence has been felt. Canadian dollars and experts helped build hospitals, technical schools and universities, agricultural research stations, family planning clinics, hydroelectric plants, and irrigation and fresh water systems. Canadian universities trained the specialists necessary to run them. And whenever needed, Canadian food helped to feed the undernourished. By the early 1990s some of that aid was being redirected towards Russia and the newly independent countries of the old Soviet Empire, as they teetered on the brink of economic and social collapse.

Canada is also part of the Americas, but has repeatedly rejected the idea of joining the Organization of American States (OAS), a regional association formed in 1948 and composed of the United States and twenty other Central and South American republics. Canadians did not see their country as part of the Americas in 1948 and, more importantly, successive governments feared that Canada would simply become the tail on the American dog, with no ability to influence the dog's behaviour. However, in 1970 Canada accepted an "observer" status in the OAS, and in 1989 Prime Minister Mulroney announced that Canada would officially join the Organization. The negotiations for the North American Free Trade Agreement with the United States and Mexico in 1993, which could ultimately be expanded to include nations of South America, further tightened Canada's economic and political relations in the Americas.

The Pacific Rim, Prime Minister Trudeau once said, should not be thought of as the "Far East," but rather, as Canada's "New West." The reason, of course, was economic opportunity, for there had never been close cultural or political ties with the nations of the Pacific. But by the 1960s Japan had emerged from the ashes of Hiroshima and Nagasaki and was on its way to becoming a major industrial and financial power. By 1973 Japan had become Canada's second largest trading partner, and throughout the 1970s and 1980s Canadian diplomats worked hard to strengthen economic, political, and cultural ties with Japan. Diplomats and businesspeople also payed increasing attention to the smaller Pacific nations—Korea, Taiwan, and Singapore, among others—who were making the Rim the most dynamic region in the world economy. And the possibilities for trade and investment in mainland China seemed boundless.

Canada had toyed with the idea of recognizing Communist China in the 1960s but, faced with American opposition, had always drawn back. After his election in 1968, however, Prime Minister Trudeau was determined to end the folly and, after months of delicate negotiations, Canada and China established diplomatic relations. Ironically, in this situation, where Canada led, the United States soon followed.

Although Canada had established a presence in its "New West," the relationship had been almost exclusively economic. On the streets of Vancouver, Toronto, and Montreal, however, the people of the New West are now strikingly present.

Canada is also a Northern nation, sharing an Arctic border with the Soviet Union, the United States, Iceland, Finland, and the Scandinavian countries. Until the end of the Cold War, the circumpolar North was the route missiles would follow, and American and Soviet submarines played hide-and-seek beneath the deep polar ice. Sovereignty over this vast territory of water and floating ice was always disputed, particularly by the Americans who claimed, in particular, that the narrow Northwest Passage was an international waterway. But in 1970, to protect the fragile environment and its own interests, Canada declared a 100-mile Arctic pollution zone and a 200-mile economic zone (as on other coasts). The Americans were enraged, but all other Arctic nations, including the Soviet Union, supported the Canadian decision. Since the end

In 1969, when the American supertanker, the *USS Manhattan,* attempted to crash through the ice in the narrow Northwest Passage, Canadians were disturbed by the threat to the fragile environment and the apparent disregard for Canadian sovereignty over the Passage. Duncan Macpherson of the *Toronto Star* captured the Canadian mood.

of the Cold War, there has been increased Russian–Canadian and multilateral collaboration to protect the environment. And in 1989, for the first time, the Soviet Inuit were allowed to attend a conference of other northern peoples.

Geography and history may have contributed to regional and cultural conflicts within Canada, but they have also combined to give Canada a rich, and sometimes tragic, experience in international affairs. Throughout the twentieth century Canada has been willing to pay the price for the peace and prosperity of the world, but few Canadians are aware of these contributions, so obsessed are they with the raking divisions within. There are some, however, such as journalist Andrew Cohen, who believe that Canada's role abroad could set an international example as we attempt to resolve some of our problems at home:

> *In the breadth of Canada's internationalism, as a leading citizen of the world, there is a deep, untapped reservoir of unity. For a people of few national symbols, divided by race, region, and language, Canada's international personality could become the vessel of a modern, pan-Canadian identity. It could transcend culture and politics. If Canadians could only see themselves as others see us—as a land of opportunity, hope and generosity—they might begin to think of themselves differently. They might find purpose, pride, and confidence. This vision, articulated vigorously by thoughtful leaders, could make Canadians become more than Quebecers, Albertans and Nova Scotians. Sadly, though, no government has used the appeal of foreign policy as an instrument of national reconciliation.*
>
> *Here, then, is the real challenge for Canada in the 1990s and beyond: to find the purpose, to create the interest, to forge the unity, to be as confident in preserving the future of Canada as Canada has been in preserving the future of the world. (*Policy Options, *July-August 1993, 81)*

12 Canada's Prime Ministers: Heroes or Villains?

LIKE SCRIPT WRITERS FOR MOVIES, some historians like to cast our twenty prime ministers as either villains or heroes. Not surprisingly, there is little agreement among them with regards to our leaders, except among those of the school that finds all politicians villains.

It is not so much the facts that divide historians as the ideological and cultural baggage that we all bring to our task. To some historians Macdonald's execution of Louis Riel was an unfortunate but necessary punishment for treason; to others it was a cowardly surrender to the furious bigotry of English Canadians; and to others it was an unconscionable punishment by a government whose incompetence had led to the rebellion. Some historians see the Canadian Pacific Railway as the fulfilment of a National Dream, others as having subjected the West to the mercy of an avaricious monopoly. Some historians condemn the process whereby Canadian leaders become successful by practising the base art of compromise and, as the historian Blair Neatby wrote, developing "a talent for smothering rather than rousing regional or cultural emotions." Others praise the political process as essential to national survival; the heroes are those who have practised it best and the villains those who have been misguided enough to place principles above consensus.

Unlike the United States or Britain, we do not seem to have any real heroes among our prime ministers. Wondering why this is so—why Canada has no Washingtons or Churchills—author Blair Neatby offers the following explanation:

> *Canada is a political creation but there is no Canadian nation. We have no common cultural heritage, no sense of dramatic collective achievement. In short we have no clear sense of identity. And without a sense of national identity, there can be no national hero. Heroes are made, not born. They are human beings who have been endowed in retrospect with heroic stature because they symbolize some central aspect of this identity.**

But perhaps we should judge our political leadership against the background of the deep cultural and regional divisions within Canadian society. Canada is not an easy country to govern, and instead of looking for heroes or villains, it may be better to review those who have led the country through its arduous 125-year journey.

Of all our leaders, Sir John A. Macdonald has probably come the closest to heroic stature. A reluctant convert to Confederation, once persuaded, his was the guiding hand that led to its completion. As prime minister for most of the next quarter century, he secured the West by purchase, consolidated it with the CPR, nourished the growth of Canadian industry with a protective tariff, fought strenuously for a strong national government, and passionately supported the existence of a Canada independent of the United States.

Jovial and earthy, Sir John A. thrived on the rough and tumble life of politics. His fondness for the bottle was legendary (and too often visible), and he acted on the maxim that every man had his price—certainly his party did when dispensing government favours. But the gifts of jobs and contracts and protective tariffs were part of the glue that held together a party containing French *nationalistes* and English

"Mackenzie King and the Historians," in *Mackenzie King: Widening the Debate*, John English and J.O. Stubbs (Toronto, 1978).

imperialists, Catholics and Protestants, industrialists and workers and farmers. Macdonald ran in six elections, and lost only one; he saw Riel's execution bring the *nationalistes* to power in Quebec and stimulate an anti-French backlash in Ontario; he heard Nova Scotians and Manitobans speak sullenly of secession; and he stood aside as Ontario urged the other provinces to rewrite the Constitution and demolish the national government. Although his party disintegrated after his death in 1891, Sir John A. had seen Canada through its first critical quarter century.

"My object," Sir Wilfrid Laurier wrote to an Ontario friend, "is to consolidate Confederation and to bring our people, long estranged from each other, gradually to become a nation. This is the supreme issue. Everything else is subordinate to that idea." Laurier had come to power when the French and the English were fighting over the destruction of French-language rights in Manitoba. He was defeated fifteen years later when the French and the English were divided over Canada's relations with the British Empire. He died soon after the end of World War I, with the two peoples more estranged than ever before. Laurier gave his name to an era of fabulous economic growth, but even though his may have been the guiding hand, it was changes in the international economy that fulfilled the promise of Sir John A.'s "National Policy."

Dignified in appearance, gentle in word and behaviour, loved by his friends, and respected by his enemies, Laurier spent his life trying to bridge the chasm between the French and the English with regards to schools, language, and the British connection. In 1911 the British asked Canada to contribute to the British navy. With English-Canadian "imperialists" demanding a large cash contribution to build a battleship, and French-Canadian nationalists determined that Canada should do nothing that would draw Canada into the vortex of European wars, Laurier countered both with the proposal to build a small Canadian navy. The "tin pot" navy proposal was rejected by both sides. At the same time, Laurier was under fire

"When this man is gone who will be there to take his place? Who else is there who knows the sheep or whose voice the sheep know?" wondered Goldwin Smith, an English historian living in Toronto at the time of Macdonald's death.

Grip, June 13, 1891.

The *Toronto News* saved this cartoon for its front page on the morning of the September 21, 1911, election.

for the reciprocity agreement, which provided for freer trade with the United States in order to assist the primary producers, particularly the farmers of Western Canada. Eastern Canadian manufacturers and financiers of both political stripes rose up to denounce reciprocity, but cloaked their self-interest—some of which was admitted—in the garb of patriotism. Reciprocity meant annexation, the end of the British connection, and the death of a British Canadian nationality.

In the election of 1911 Laurier had to fight on two fronts at once. As he said during the campaign, "I am branded in Quebec as a traitor to the French, and in Ontario as a traitor to the English. In Quebec I am branded as a Jingo, and in Ontario as a separatist. In Quebec I am attacked as an Imperialist, and in Ontario as an anti-Imperialist. I am neither, I am a Canadian." But there was no shared Canadian vision to which Laurier could appeal. He lost the election and was replaced by Robert Borden, whose Conservative government was an unholy alliance of those contradictory elements that had brought about Laurier's defeat. Six years later Laurier watched in agony and impotence as Borden formed an all English-Canadian Union government—Conservatives and Liberals—to win the 1917 election with no support from French Canada, imposing conscription, and splitting the country as it had never been before and from which it never fully recovered.

William Lyon Mackenzie King, who succeeded Laurier as Liberal leader, was prime minister throughout the 1920s and again from 1935 to 1948. If longevity was the mark of political success, King was our most successful prime minister. Historians, like his contemporaries, look in vain for grand pronouncements or dynamic policies. As his biographer, Blair Neatby, observed, they find "the great compromiser, the man who avoided confrontations, who soothed critics with soft answers, who placated dissident regions with concessions, who maintained a precarious balance by shifting ever so slightly left or right, east or west, but never far from the centre."

King was by nature cautious and conciliatory. "Government itself, in a democratic state," he wrote, "is largely concerned with overcoming and reconciling differences." And he once told his cabinet that "it is what we prevent, rather than what we do that counts most in government." King knew that a Liberal party with strength across Canada was essential to his political success. But he also believed that a broad-based party and government that could accommodate and broker the competing interests, regions, and races was the best guarantee of national unity.

Faced with a revolt of the farmers who were still smarting from the defeat of reciprocity, and who sent sixty-four Progressives to Ottawa in the election of 1921, King defused the protest by lowering the tariff and freight rates (but not enough to antagonize big business) and co-opting their leaders. By the end of the decade the farmers' movement was dead, only to re-emerge during the Depression as the CCF (the Co-operative Commonwealth Federation, which later became the New Democratic Party, or NDP) and Social Credit parties.

In 1918 Mackenzie King had written *Industry and Humanity.* The book is long on platitude and short on concrete proposals. King argued that old-fashioned laissez-faire liberalism was out of place in an urban and industrialized Canada. In the book, at least, he was prepared to see the state play a larger role and suggested more generally that "wherever, in social or industrial relations, the claims of Industry and Humanity are opposed, those of Industry must give way." Few shared King's high opinion of his work; it was, one journalist commented, a book "which more Canadians have failed to read than any other."

The Standard, Montreal, December 28, 1935.

During the 1930s King excused federal inaction on the grounds that the unemployed were a provincial responsibility. During the war he only reluctantly accepted new responsibilities for social security and greater intervention in the economy because he feared provincial opposition, particularly from Quebec. And on most matters affecting Quebec, he deferred to the views of his Quebec colleagues.

King's cautiously isolationist foreign policy between the wars not only reflected his own views, but also was designed to lighten the shadow of 1917 in Quebec. But it seemed to appeal to all but the most imperialistic Canadians and the few who believed that the League of Nations could work. He brought a more or less united nation into World War II, and lived up to his promise not to use conscription until the casualties in Europe and the pressure from English Canada forced it upon him.

King's prime ministerial career was not a heroic achievement, but as Blair Neatby concluded, if "politics is the art of the possible, politicians should be judged by what is feasible." And King's fierce critic Frank Underhill admitted that "Mr. King for twenty-five years was the leader who divided us least." From the perspective of 1994 that is not a bad obituary.

King's legacy was a party that remained in power for almost a decade under his successor, Louis St. Laurent. A corporation lawyer before he entered politics, St. Laurent let powerful ministers, such as C. D. Howe, run the government, while he made annual reports to the nation much as a company president would to the shareholders. But the Liberals had grown too accustomed to power, too convinced they had a "divine right" to govern, too insensitive to the grievances of the poorer shareholders of the nation. In 1957 they were defeated by John Diefenbaker's Conservatives.

Diefenbaker was a prophet and politics was his pulpit. A Prairie courtroom lawyer with a commanding appearance, he moved the national jury with passion not substance, with "visions of opportunity," not policies. But once in office Diefenbaker found that a recession and unemployment, Quebec nationalism and provincial discontent, and American criticisms of his ambiguous defence policy were not solved by oratorical outbursts. His unhyphenated Canadianism had no appeal in Quebec, and his nostalgia for the British connection seemed strangely out of date. His government was not without its accomplishments, but they were episodic and fragmented. Five years after being elected in 1958 with the greatest majority in Canadian history, he was defeated in 1963 by the Liberal party led by Lester Pearson. Quebec and the cities deserted him; only rural Canada kept the faith. The prophet had failed to master the art of governing.

"Mike" Pearson was more the beneficiary of the collapse of the Diefenbaker government than of a groundswell of support among the people. In 1963 and again in 1965 he was not able to win a majority. Pearson did not look or act like a politician and, in fact, he was not a very good one. The most notable accomplishments of his administration were old age pensions and medicare. But he had neither initiative nor determination, and although his diplomatic skills were useful in resolving divisions within his cabinet and overcoming the opposition of the provinces, the advocates of progressive social legislation in the cabinet found his caution and indecision frustrating and his habit of seeing too many sides to every question unprincipled.

Pearson's failure to stem the tide of nationalism in Quebec was less a comment on his well-meaning intentions or resolution than on the growing polarization of opinion in the country. The sensible appointment of a Royal Commission on Bilingualism and Biculturalism was attacked by Premier Manning (father of Reform party leader, Preston) of Alberta as implying some form of special status for the French language and culture. When Pearson agreed that Quebec (and other provinces if they wished) could formally opt out of shared-cost programs he was accused of "balkanizing" the country. Many Tories agreed with the description in the *Vancouver Province* of the new flag with the red maple leaf—

"A simple Yes or No will suffice."

Lester Pearson had promised to secure a distinctive Canadian flag that did not reflect our colonial past as did the Red Ensign, which included the Union Jack. Diefenbaker spoke for many Canadians who wanted to retain the Union Jack in some way, and who believed that the maple leaf flag was simply another way of appeasing Quebec. After months of debate, the flag was finally approved and became the national flag in 1965. "O Canada" was approved as the national anthem in 1967 in time for the country's 100th birthday.

Reprinted with permission—*The Toronto Star* Syndicate.

which Pearson hoped would be a symbol of both nationhood and national unity—as a symbol "of disunity," and "of Ottawa's pandering to Quebec." And when Pearson began the process of constitutional reform, the warning came from Western Canada that if it was intended to lead to any special status for Quebec it was doomed to failure.

On the other hand, when General Charles de Gaulle came to Canada in 1967 to encourage Quebec separatists with his infamous "Vive le Québec libre" speech, Pearson's strong censure of the French leader's statement was universally praised in English Canada. While Quebec nationalists were singularly unimpressed by Pearson's diplomacy, some federalists in Quebec had concluded that ultranationalism had to be fought rather than appeased. In the 1965 election three of them—Jean Marchand, Gérard Pelletier, and Pierre Trudeau—were elected as Liberal MPs. Worn out and perhaps depressed by his limited success, Pearson resigned in 1968. To the surprise of many the Liberal mantle fell on Pierre Trudeau.

Trudeau personally, perhaps more than any other prime minister in our history, dominated the political scene for the next sixteen years, and he is still a very powerful presence. His style suited the young and urban Canadian of the 1960s, who found the freewheeling bachelor (who soon married a twenty-two-year-old flower child) and outspoken intellectual a refreshing change from the greybeards who usually ran the country. But in time the image was tarnished by Trudeau's displays of arrogance and contemptuous dismissal of those who dared to disagree with him. He preferred to practise the politics of confrontation, and regarded compromise as weak and unprincipled, grudgingly resorting to it only as a last resort. No one was indifferent to Pierre Trudeau while he was in office. Even a decade later objectivity remains difficult as we still live in the shadow cast by his career.

Pierre Trudeau's goal was to undermine the appeal of ultranationalism and separatism in Quebec by offering the alternatives of national bilingualism and the Charter of Rights and Freedoms. Although he remained firmly in control of Quebec on the federal level and helped defeat the separatist referendum, the Parti Québécois was victorious on the provincial scene. While Trudeau encouraged the rest of Canada to endorse bilingualism, arousing an intense backlash in Western Canada, both the PQ and the provincial Liberals endorsed official unilingualism in Quebec.

We can only speculate on what might have happened if the separatists had entered federal politics while Trudeau was prime minister. All we know is that ten years later when they did enter federal politics they won fifty-four of Quebec's seventy-five seats in 1993. Nationalism became the dominant ideology in Quebec and made the constitutional status quo increasingly unacceptable, even if independence was too fearful for many to

The candidate

Trudeau had been narrowly defeated in 1979, but the Conservatives, led by Joe Clark, did not win a majority in the Commons. The Clark government was soon defeated in the Commons over their proposed tax on gasoline, and a new election was held. The Liberals realized that Trudeau, personally, was not very popular, and his advisers urged him to keep a very low profile. The strategy worked.

Reprinted with permission—*The Toronto Star* Syndicate.

support. Trudeau's boast, when he emerged from retirement to fight Meech Lake, that his 1982 Constitution "was set to last a thousand years!" indeed set a new level for hyperbole.

If Trudeau helped keep Quebec in Canada, he also forced some western Canadians to think of secession. The Liberals had not been strong in the West since Diefenbaker. The infectious "Trudeaumania" in 1968 gave him thirty-seven percent of the vote and twenty-seven seats west of Ontario. But his language policy (often misunderstood), his alleged indifference to western interests, and above all his energy policies, which hurt the oil- and gas-producing provinces, alienated western Canadians. In 1980 less than one in four westerners voted for him and the Liberals were reduced to a pitiful two seats in Winnipeg. By the mid-1970s the western provinces, led by Alberta, were also demanding changes to the Constitution that would reduce the power of the federal government. A decade later the Reform party had emerged to articulate all the grievances of the West, and in 1993 won fifty-one of the eighty-six western seats. That, too, in part, was Trudeau's legacy.

Yet without Trudeau the advocates of decentralization might have fatally weakened the federal government. Trudeau fought for a Canada that was more than the sum of its provincial and cultural parts, that was more than "a community of communities." He resisted provincial demands for more power and Quebec's demand for special status. Rather, he attempted to break down interprovincial and intercultural barriers and established a basis of common Canadianism with the Charter of Rights and Freedoms. That, also, was his bequest to the nation.

Few men could be more dissimilar than Pierre Trudeau and Brian Mulroney. Trudeau, the millionaire's son from Montreal, entered politics with a well-defined political philosophy. Mulroney, the electrician's son from Baie Comeau, entered politics with a well-connected network of friends. Ever since he entered college Mulroney had been obsessed with politics, and in 1976, at age thirty-seven, he ran for the Tory leadership even though he had never even contested a seat in Parliament.

Mulroney lost that first campaign to Joe Clark, but from his office as president of the Iron Ore Company, he spent much of the next seven years building up his political contacts. Although he publicly supported Joe Clark as Tory

After Mulroney's 1984 sweep, a rump of forty Liberals and thirty New Democrats faced 211 Tories in the Commons. The biggest surprise was the return of sixty-three Tories in Quebec, where Mulroney had fashioned an alliance with the nationalists—an alliance that was to come back to haunt him.

Reprinted with permission—*The Toronto Star* Syndicate.

leader, privately he is said to have been undermining him. When Clark called a leadership review convention in 1983, Mulroney ran against him and won. A year later, when Trudeau's successor, John Turner, went to the people, Mulroney's Conservatives won 211 of the 282 seats in Parliament; a landslide, second only to Diefenbaker's in 1958. Four years later, in an election fought largely on free trade, Mulroney again won comfortably. But with the defeat of the Charlottetown Accord and the polls revealing his declining popularity, Brian Mulroney resigned in 1993.

Canadian voters gave their verdict on Mulroney in the election of October 1993. When he left office the polls showed that he was supported by only sixteen percent of the population. Conservative popularity improved dramatically under what appeared to be the refreshing leadership of his successor, Kim Campbell. But with her own shortcomings increasingly evident, Campbell could not dispel the dark shadows left by her predecessor, and on October 25 the grand old party of John A. Macdonald was left with only two seats—and a meagre sixteen percent of the popular vote. It was the greatest political defeat in Canadian history.

Most historians have already delivered their opinions on Brian Mulroney, but they have done so as observers and participants, not as scholars. Unlike most economists, many Canadian historians were opposed to the Free Trade Agreement with the United States, and then with Mexico, that Mulroney fought for so diligently. Like the opponents of reciprocity in 1911 these historians either feared for their country or were by nature and training anti-American. Historians who opposed Meech Lake and Charlottetown—and unlike the political scientists they were undoubtedly in the majority—hailed Mulroney's defeat on both counts. However, when it comes to such matters as the privatization of government agencies, the goods and services tax, or determining the best balance between government deficits and social spending, the historian is, at best, only an educated commentator. In the end, history may not be kind to Brian Mulroney, and if not, it may not be due to his policies. History may conclude, as have some of his contemporaries, that the poor boy from Baie Comeau was not guided by principle, but driven by an ambition and vanity so great that he ultimately could not be trusted.

For better or for worse these are the eight prime ministers who have left their footsteps in the sands of Canadian history. The other twelve, who held office for a total of eighteen of our 127 years, were neither villains nor heroes, and several had long and fruitful careers in federal politics. Perhaps leaders such as Alexander Mackenzie, Sir John Abbott, Sir Mackenzie Bowell, Robert Borden, and R. B. Bennett deserve better than omission, here, as do Sir John Thompson, Sir Charles Tupper, Arthur Meighen, John Turner, and Joe Clark. Certainly historians will long debate why, after a seemingly auspicious beginning, Kim Campbell led the Progressive Conservative party to the greatest defeat in the history of Canada, and conceivably to its extinction. And Jean Chrétien's place in Canadian history will depend upon whether he is the last Québécois to be prime minister of Canada.

Epilogue: Where Are We?

IF NOTHING CHANGED, there would be no history. Historians like to write about eras of transition and events that mark turning points on our way to the present. Canada is undergoing such an era of transition today; we have reached a turning point in our history that can best be described as the day of reckoning. It's time to pay the bills and assess the future.

Decades of almost unbroken growth and prosperity enabled Canada and the Western World to embark on an adventure that has now come to close. Here and elsewhere, western countries are staggering under debts that were once unimaginable outside of wartime. Unemployment levels—ours are among the worst—have soared to heights not seen since the Great Depression of the 1930s. Tens of millions live on public welfare. Costly programs to care for the sick, support the old, and educate the young are under seige. Taxes have risen to the point where many Canadians have joined the "underground economy" to escape paying taxes. Every opinion survey taken shows that where once we expected that life would get better and better, we are now apprehensive—or even certain—that it will get worse and worse. Consequently, many of us long for the good old days.

But the good old days as we knew them are gone forever. We will have to learn, as a country and as individuals, to live a leaner life. Since 1945 Canadians have built a high-cost country with one of the best health care systems, one of the most generous social welfare programs—second only to Sweden in support for single-parent families, for example—and one of the most expensive educational systems in the world. We have spent generously on culture, gracing our urban landscapes with galleries and concert halls, Olympic stadiums and Skydomes.

Alas, we must now pay the bills. As a nation we must bring our expectations into line with our capacity to pay. In the end, a country, like a family, can only consume what it can pay for. For the past twenty years Canada has spent more than it has made in every single year. Debt has risen faster than economic growth. In fact, our accumulated debt of all levels of government is now ninety-seven percent of the worth of the entire economy (or GDP). Put more personally, if the debt were to be paid off by the Canadian people today, it would cost each Canadian almost $25,000. The interest on the Canadian debt is $40 billion a year, which means that out of every dollar the government takes in it spends thirty-four cents just to pay the interest. To make matters worse, there is always a danger that lenders will either increase the interest charges or refuse to loan us any more money.

The problem is that few Canadians want to pay their share of the bill. Arts groups and the CBC claim that Canadian culture is the "glue" that holds the country together, and if their support is reduced the country will come "unstuck." Doctors and health professionals warn that cuts to their income will destroy health care. Welfare advocates insist that any reduction in benefits is a merciless attack on the unfortunate. Professors and teachers argue that freezing their salaries will jeopardize the education of the young. Students protest that having to pay a larger share of the real cost of their education will force them to leave university. Ordinary Canadians, staggering under the burden of heavy taxes, point their finger at the corporations, the rich, or simply, the others.

The severity of this unsustainable situation is in part, but only in part, the result of the recessions of the 1980s and

1990s. The slowdown in economic growth simultaneously reduced government income, for there was less to tax, and increased government expenditure, particularly for unemployment and welfare benefits. The long-run solution lies in restoring economic growth. In the short-run, at least, costs must be controlled and cut.

But a real economic recovery will depend on an economic transformation. For decades there has been a massive shift from labour-intensive to knowledge-intensive occupations. Whereas at one time most Canadians worked in "goods producing" jobs—manufacturing, forestry, agriculture—today, seventy-five percent work in the service sector, and while that includes McDonald's, it also includes banking and finance, the professions, research labs, and other knowledge-intensive activities. Moreover, even in the goods-producing sector, computers, robots, and complex machines are replacing men and women. In fact, many of the jobs lost during the recent recessions will never return. Thus, the workforce of the future must be much better educated if Canada is to succeed in the highly demanding global economy—and if Canadians want to get and keep jobs.

This means that there must be radical improvements in our educational system. Canada spends more money on education per capita than any other western country—Canadian teachers are among the best paid in the world—but the product bears little relationship to the investment. Canadian students are continually outperformed in international tests. The high level of illiteracy—both numerical and verbal—has led to demands for a national war on illiteracy. We have among the lowest percentage of seventeen-year-olds in school in the West, and the highest drop-out rate. But widespread demands for educational reform—higher standards, a more rigorous curriculum, and discipline—meet with opposition from the educational bureaucracy who, after all, have created the system, and as its keepers seem strangely blind to the real needs of those who are inside it.

"The only way to get a high school education," one writer quipped, "is to go to university." But the universities also seem incapable of combining a traditional liberal education with a practical component more directed towards the job market, and are overwhelmed by the task of dealing with a student population that is often ill equipped to tackle university studies. Caught in the three-way trap of a financial squeeze, the monetary demands and protective tactics of a unionized faculty, and a mandate of accessibility and equality for all, academic quality in the ivory tower is deteriorating rapidly.

Yet improving education is only a partial solution. The changing nature of the economy and the economic slowdown has hit young people much harder than their parents. A report by Statistics Canada in March 1994 pointed to the alarming increase in unemployment among fifteen- to twenty-four-year-olds, and among those in that age group who have never had a job and have not developed the skills or the discipline to get one. Experts speak despairingly of a "lost generation" whose future looks bleak, but we cannot afford the human or economic costs of a lost generation.

The years leading up to the twenty-first century will be difficult ones for Canadians—more difficult than any since the 1930s. Canadians tend to lay the blame for their misfortunes on governments, but governments are caught in the grip of forces over which they often have only minimal control, and are also merely the mirror of those who elect them. Ultimately, it will only be the development of a sense of national purpose, a strong sense of community among people who are willing to share the sacrifices that must be made, and imaginative leadership in the private and public sectors that will carry Canada through these difficult years of transition. Without stability and prosperity at home, our continued efforts to act as "peacekeeper to the world," to aid the impoverished worldwide, and to protect the environment will be crippled. To say that we have overcome threats to our unity and even survival in the past does not solve our present discontents. To conclude that we cannot meet the internal and international challenges to our future would be a tragedy. What is now necessary is a reaffirmation in attitudes and policies of the importance and value of being Canadian.

Index

A
Aberhart, William, 48
aboriginal people:
  arrival from Siberia, 9
  in the North, 9
  population 1881, 9
  rights and Constitution, 105
abortion:
  Charter case, 122
  law, 66
Acadia, 5, 6
  war over, 22
affirmative action, 58
Africa, immigration from, 13
agriculture, 44
  land under cultivation, 4
Alaska, 36
Alberta, 35
Alberta Compulsory Arbitration Act, Charter case, 121
American Civil War, 30-1
American Revolution, 24-5
  population movement after, 26
Americanization, fear of, 56
Amerindians, pre-contact population size, 9
Amin, Idi, 14
Anne of Green Gables, 5
annexation, 56
  of British North America, 32
Appalachian Mountains, 5
Arctic region:
  area of, 9
  economic zone, 139
  pollution zone, 139
  population of, 9, 11
  submarines in, 139
Asia, immigration from, 13
Assiniboine, and settlement of West, 39
Atlantic provinces, 5
  and immigration, 6
Auto Pact (1965), 52

B
backbenchers, 63-4, 66
Bengough, J.W., 75, 88
Bering Sea, bridge, 9
bilingualism, 94, 152
Bill 101, Quebec, 115
birthrate, Quebec, 84
Bloc Québécois, 108, 110-11
Boer War, 89
Borden, Robert, 146-7
Bosnia, 133-4
Bouchard, Lucien, 111
  cartoon, 108
Bourassa, Henri, 89
Bourassa, Robert, 95, 102, 107, 109
  cartoon, 103
Bourassa government, and notwithstanding clause, 115
"branch plant economy" concern, 44
breathalyser tests, Charter case, 123
Britain. *See* Great Britain
British Columbia:
  acquisition of, 36-7
  hydroelectric power in, 8
British Commonwealth of Nations, 137
British Empire, change to Commonwealth of Nations, 128
British North America Act, 1867. *See* Constitution, 1867
Brock, Isaac, 27
buffalo, and Plains Indians, 10, 39-40
Butler, Donald Victor, 120

C
cabinet, federal, 61, 63
"Call Off The Party" (Kilgour), 66
Campbell, Kim, 156-7
"Canada round" of constitutional reform, 109
Canada-US:
  boundary, 28
  relations, 135
  See also United States
Canadian Army and Air Force, in Germany, 135
Canadian Charter of Rights and Freedoms. *See* Charter of Rights and Freedoms
Canadian Multicultural Act, 14
Canadian National Railway, 47
Canadian Pacific Railway, 38, 142
Canadian Shield, 7
capital city, choosing of, 34
Cartier, Jacques, discovery of St. Lawrence, 19
  map, 18
CBC (Canadian Broadcasting Corporation), 159
CCF (Co-operative Commonwealth Federation), 147
census, 1881, population size of Indians, 9
Chambers, cartoonist, 103
Champlain, Samuel de, 19
Charlottetown Accord, 71-2, 109, 111-12, 156
Charlottetown, and confederation, 34
Charter of Rights and Freedoms (1982), 13, 69, 105, 113, 152, 154
  language rights, 101
  and litigation, 116-25
  opposition to, 114-15
  sample text, 117
  and Supreme Court, 116, 125
children, of immigrants, 15
China. *See* Communist China
Chrétien, Jean, 58, 68, 110, 157
Churchill Falls, 51
Churchill, Winston, 134
circumpolar North, 139
civil servants, 61
Clark, Joe, 104, 153, 155-6
Clarkson, Mrs., Charter case, 121-2
Clinton, President, 58
Cohen, Andrew, 141
Cold War, 134-5, 139
Colombo Plan, 137
colonization, early attempts, 17
"colour-blind" immigration policy, 13
Columbia River, 51
commercial system, collapse of, 29
Commonwealth Air Training Plan, 129
Commonwealth of Nations, 128, 137
Communist China, 135, 139
confederation, negotiation of, 34, 73-4
confederation. *See also* Constitution
Congress, role of, 60-1
Conservative party, 46, 56, 68, 146-7, 149, 153, 156
  annihilation of, 110
  caucus, 66
constituencies, 67
constitution:
  American model, 74
  provincial powers in, 87
  reform of, 70, 100
  unwritten, 63
Constitution Act:
1867, 34, 53, 69, 76, 77, 86, 87
  amending formula, 102
  patriation of, 101
  1940 amendment, 54, 79
  1982, 79, 105, 154
  and the Charter, 118
Continental Congress (Philadelphia, 1774), 24-5
coureurs de bois, 19
Courts, and federal-provincial relationships, 76
Cree:
  compensation to, 7
  and settlement of West, 39
Criminal Code, Charter cases, 120, 122-3
Cross, James, 96
Cuban missile crisis, 135
cultural mosaic, 13-14
cultures, conflict of, 87

D
Davey, Keith, 98
de Gaulle, Charles, 152
de la Salle, Cavelier, 21
debt, accumulated, 159
deficits, government, 54, 59, 80, 158
Delatri, cartoonist, 115
Depression. *See* Great Depression
Desert Storm, 133, 136
Diefenbaker, John, 135, 149, 151
distinct society, Quebec as, 107
Donato, Andy, 124
drinking and driving, and Charter, 125
drought, prairie, 47
Duplessis, Maurice, 92, 113
Durham, Lord, 86, 89

E
economic development:
  of the North, 11
  and provincial governments, 77
  and World War I, 45
economic expansion:
  in 1920s, 47, 51
  as National Policy, 38
economic growth, 42, 54, 159-60
  postwar boom, 51
economic zone, Arctic region, 139
economy:
  reconstruction of, 59
  weaknesses in, 56
education, 79, 87, 159-61
  French-language schools, 89, 94
  in Quebec, 90-1, 92
elections:
  and campaigns, 68
  and democratic process, 68
  federal (1980), 67-8
  federal (1988), 68
  New Brunswick (1987), 67
electricity, household use of, 47
  See also hydroelectric power
Elizabeth, Queen, 106
Emery's Bar, *illustration*, 33
energy policies, Liberal government, 154
  See also oil and gas resources
English, as language of business, 89, 91
English-Canadian Union government, 147
English-French hostility, 90
environment, and Russian-Canadian collaboration, 140
equalization payments, 79-80
  and Constitution, 105
"ethnic cleansing," 133
European:
  settlement, 8, 11-12
  wars and French Canada, 144
European Economic Community (EEC), 56
expansionism, fear of American, 32, 34
exploration:
  early, 19
  westward, 21
export industries, 47, 51

F
farmers, and politics, 46, 147
farming:
  in Ontario, 7
  Prairie provinces, 8
  Prince Edward Island, 5
  in Quebec, 7
  See also agriculture
Fathers of Confederation, 73, 87
federal government:
  as centralized system, 75-6
  powers of, 74
federal-provincial negotiations, 81-2
federalism:
  and the provinces, 75
  and Quebec, 95
Filion, Gérard, 91
First Nations people, 9
fishing, Atlantic, 5, 59
flag issue, 150-1
foreign aid, and Third World, 137-8
foreign investment, 43-4
foreign policy:
  control of, by Great Britain, 126-8
  isolationist, 149
  and US, 135-6
forest industry, 5-6
forty-ninth parallel, 28
France, immigration from, 19

Fraser River, 33
free trade:
adopted by Britain, 29-30
election issue, 68-9, 156
with United States, 30, 42, 44, 56
Free Trade Agreement (FTA), 57-8, 156
free votes, in Parliament, 66
Freedom of Association, Charter case, 121
Freedom of Expression, Charter cases, 120-1
freight rates, 147
French:
and Indian War, 21-2
language rights in Manitoba, 87, 144
as official language in Quebec, 98, 115
French Canadians, 11
and industrialization, 90
outside Quebec, 6, 83
in Quebec, 7
survival of, 83, 86
French-English conflict, 84
and Boer War, 89
and Louis Riel, 42
Front de Libération du Québec (FLQ), 85, 96
fur trade, 31

G
Ganges (immigrant ship), 12
global economy, 56
Globe and Mail, 134
gold:
discovery of, in Fraser River, 33
in South Africa, 42
in Yukon, 42
mining, in Manitoba, 8
golden horseshoe, 7
goods, production of, 58, 160
goods and services tax (GST), 66, 80
Governor General, role of, 61, 63
Grand Trunk Railway, 30
Great Britain:
and American Civil War, 31
independence from, 128
migration from, 11
Great Depression, 47-8, 53-4, 78-9, 147
and immigration, 11
Great Recession (1980s), 54
Great Western Railway, 30
Gross Domestic Product (GDP), 53, 80
Group of Seven (G7) nations, 53, 56

H
Harper, Elijah, 107
hate propaganda, Charter case, 120
health care system, 79, 158-9
See also hospital insurance; medicare
historians, opinions of, 156-7
Hitler, Adolf, 48, 129
hospital insurance, 54, 79
House of Commons, 61, 64, 71
Howe, C.D., 149
Hudson Bay, war over, 22
Hudson's Bay Company, land holdings, 31-2, 34-5
human rights, 113
commissions, 116
Hussein, Saddam, 133
hydroelectric power, 43, 51
in British Columbia, 8
and Canadian Shield, 7
and economic expansion, 50-1

I
illiteracy, 160
immigrants, and language, 115
immigration:
backlash to, 14
change prior to World War I, 11
debate about, 15
from Asia, 13
from Great Britain, 6, 28
from Latin America, 13
from Third World countries, 13
public opinion survey about, 14-15
to 1850, 28
Impaired Driving, Charter case, 123, 125
Imperial Conference:
1923, 128
1926, 128
imperial preference, 28-9
imports, 56

income tax:
personal, 80
and provinces, 77, 80-1
independence, threat to, from US, 53
India, independence of, 137
Indian people, 9-11
and settlement of West, 39
See also aboriginal people
industrial society, Canada as, 44, 49
industrialization:
in Quebec, 90
and the railways, 30
Industry and Humanity (King), 148
inflation (1970s), 54
integration, as National Policy, 38
International Francophonie, 137
Inuit:
in Arctic region, 9, 11
compensation to, 7
invasion, fear of American, 32
"iron curtain," 134
iron ore, 50
Iron Ore Company, 155
isolation, policy of, 128-9
Israel, and Egypt conflict, 131-2

J
James Bay, and hydroelectric power, 7, 51
Jamestown, founding of, 17
Japan:
as industrial power, 56
as trading partner, 138-9
Johnson, President, 135
Jolliet, Louis, 21
Judicial Committee (London, England), 76-7
judiciary, and the Charter, 114, 116

K
Keegstra, James, 120
Kennedy, President, 135
kidnapping:
of James Cross, 96
of Pierre Laporte, 96
Kilgour, David, 66
King, Mackenzie, 12, 128, 147, 149
cartoon, 78, 148
King government, 130
Korea, and United Nations, 131
Kumar, Prem, 15
Kuwait, and war with Iraq, 133

L
land, purchase of, by Canada, 35
language rights:
and Charter, 113
in Constitution, 87, 101
Laporte, Pierre, 96
Laskin, Bora, 124
"Last Spike" *illustration*, 39
Late Loyalists, 26
Latin America, immigration from, 13
Laurier, Sir Wilfrid, 42, 44, 89, 144, 146-7
cartoon, 67
laws, power to pass, 34
League of Nations, 127-9, 149
Lévesque, René, 95-7, 99, 106, 115
cartoon, 106
Lévesque government, 98
Liberal party, 46, 68, 110, 149, 154
Quebec, 91-2, 95, 96, 153
lieutenant-governors, provincial, 74-5
"lost generation," 161
Lougheed, Premier, 103
Lower Canada. *See* Quebec
lumber, 29, 42-3
See also forest industry

M
McCain's, 5
Macdonald, Sir John A., 34, 38, 69, 143-4
cartoon, 75
and Louis Riel, 40-2, 142, 144
Mackenzie, William Lyon, 86
McClung, Nellie, 62
Macpherson, Duncan, 140
Manicougan-Outard Rivers, 51
mandarins, 61, 63
Manifest Destiny concept, 30, 32
Manitoba:
and French language rights, 87, 144
province of, 35
Manning, Premier, 150
Manning, Preston, 72, 111, 150

manufacturing, 43-5
in Ontario, 7
Mao Zedong, 131
maps, early Canadian, 18, 20, 23
Marchand, Jean, 152
Marquette, Father, 21
medicare, 54-5, 79-80, 150
Meech Lake Accord, 107-9, 154
Métis, 10-11, 32, 35
revolt in the West, 40-1, 87
mining:
Northern Ontario, 7
Prairie provinces, 8
money, and election campaigns, 68
Montcalm, 22
Montmorency, 22
Montreal, and fur trade, 21
Morgentaler, Henry, Charter case, 66, 122-3
Mowat, Oliver, 76
Mulroney, Brian, 56-7, 68, 106-7, 138, 154-7
cartoon, 111
Mulroney government, 14, 58, 156
multiculturalism, 13
debate about, 15

N
NAFTA (North American Free Trade Agreement), 58, 138
Napoleonic Wars, 27-8
Narcotics Control Act, 119
national anthem, 151
National Citizens' Coalition, 69
National Dream, 142
National Energy Program, 52
National Policy, 38, 42, 44, 47, 144
nationalism, in Quebec, 93, 150, 152-3
Native people. *See* aboriginal people
NATO (North Atlantic Treaty Organization), 135
natural resources:
demand for, 47, 50-1
under pressure, 59
Neatby, Blair, 142-3, 147, 149
Nelson River, 51
New Democratic Party (NDP), 147
New France. *See* Quebec
Niagara Peninsula, 7
Nixon, President, *cartoon*, 136
Nobel Peace Prize:
Pearson (1957), 126
UN peacekeepers (1988), 133
nonregistered Indians, 10-11
NORAD (North American Aerospace Defence Command), 135
North. *See* Arctic region
North American Free Trade Agreement. *See* NAFTA
North Atlantic Treaty Organization. *See* NATO
Northwest Mounted Police, 40
Northwest Passage, 139, 140
notwithstanding clause, Charter, 114, 115
Nova Scotia, and American Revolution, 24-5
nuclear power, 50

O
"O Canada," national anthem, 151
Oakes, David, 119
obscene material, Charter case, 120
October crisis, 1970, 85
Official Languages Act, 93
oil and gas resources, 5, 8, 50
and Constitution, 102-3
prices, 54
US ownership of, 52
oil shock, 103
Ojibwa, and settlement of West, 39
old age pension plan, 54, 79, 150
Ontario:
American population in, in 1812, 26
early map, 20
union with Quebec, 32-3
Operation Desert Storm, 133, 136
Organization of American States (OAS), 138
organizations, and campaign funding, 68-9
Ottawa, as capital, 34

P
Pacific Rim, 138-9
Papineau, Louis Joseph, 85

parliamentary system, 60-1, 72
Parti Québécois, 95-7, 107, 108, 152
patriation of Constitution, 101
pay equity, 59
Peace River, 51
"peacekeeping" operations, 131-4
Pearson, Lester (Mike), 93, 126, 132, 134, 135, 150-2
  cartoon, 151
  and the flag, 150
Pearson government, 93, 101
Pelletier, Gérard, 152
Permanent Joint Board of Defence, 135
personal income tax, 80
Peterson, Roy, 65
pipelines, 50
Plains Indians, 10, 39-40
police action, and the Charter, 118
politicians, public attitude to, 72
politics, in Quebec, 84
pollution zone, Arctic region, 139
population:
  aboriginal people, 9-11
  by 1850, 28
  Canada, 4-5
  growth to 1914, 44
  mid-eighteenth century, 17
possession of narcotics, Charter case, 119
potash, 50
potato farming, 5
power of disallowance, 76
Prairie provinces, settlement of, 8
President (US), role of, 60-1
Presumption of Innocence, Charter case, 119
prime minister, role of, 61, 63
productivity, 56
Progressive party, 46, 147
Prosperity Certificate, 48
provinces, powers of, 74
provincial rights, 76

Q
Quebec:
  and American Revolution, 24-5
  and Constitution Act, 1982, 105-6
  early map, 23
  English-speaking minority in, 83
  farming in, 7
  independence, 83, 95, 152
  and shared-cost programs, 81-2
  special status of, 93, 95, 101
  union with Ontario, 32-3
Quebec Act (1774), 24, 84
Quebec City, 19
Quebec-Canada: A New Deal, 99
question period, 64
"Quiet Revolution," 92

R
Race Relations Directorate, Ministry of Multiculturalism, 14
racial conflict, in Quebec, 86, 89
racial discrimination, 12-14
racism, 15-16
"Racism. It's up to you" 1994 poster campaign, 16
Radio-Canada, and FLQ manifesto, 96
railways, 30
  building of, 43
  transcontinental, 38
ranching, Prairie provinces, 8
Reagan, President, 57
rebellion:
  Patriotes 1837, 85
  in Upper Canada, 86
Reciprocity Agreement, 31, 44-6, 146
reconstruction of economy, 59
Red Chinese Army, 131
Red River, and the Métis, 35
referendum:
  October 26, 1992, 109-10
  Quebec, 97, 99, 152
Reform Party, 72, 110-12, 150, 154
refugees, Canada as haven for, 14
Reid, Escott, 134
religious rights, 87
representation, unequal in Commons, 70
reserves, Indian, 10
  life on, 40
responsible government, 63
Revolutionary War. *See* American Revolution
ridings, 67
Riel, Louis, 35-6, 40-2, 88-9

and Macdonald, 142
Right to Counsel, Charter case, 121-2
Right to Life, Liberty, and Security of the Person, Charter case, 122-3
Right to strike, Charter case, 121
"Roaring Twenties," 47
Roosevelt, President, 135
Royal Commission on Bilingualism and Biculturalism, 150
Russian-Canadian collaboration, 140

S
St. Laurent, Louis, 134-5, 149
St. Lawrence Seaway, 50
St. Lawrence waterway, 7, 29
San Francisco Conference, 1945, 130
San Jacinto (warship), 31
Sarajevo, 134
Saskatchewan, 35
scrum, 65
self-government, provincial right to, 76
Senate, 57
  reform, 70-1, 107
  role of, 69-70
separatism, 93, 95
separatist referendum, 152
service sector, 44-5, 47, 58, 160
settlement, of West, early, 31-2
shared-cost programs, 79, 81, 93, 107, 150
Siberia, and aboriginal people, 9
slavery, 30
Smith, Goldwin, 145
Smuts, General, 128
social assistance. *See* welfare
Social Credit party, 48, 147
social reform, lack of, in Quebec, 91
social security system, 53, 55, 79-80, 149
Somalia, 133, 136
  war in, 14
sovereignty-association, 95, 99
special status, for Quebec, 93, 101
standard of living, Quebec, 90
Statistics Canada, 161
Statute of Westminster, 1931, 128
submarines, in Arctic region, 139
Suez Canal, 131-2
suffragettes, 62
Sumner, Charles, 32
Supreme Court of Canada, 76
  appointments to, 102, 107
  and the Charter, 114, 115, 119
  and Constitution, 105

T
tariff barriers, 38, 47, 147
Tarte, Israel, 67
taxation, 54-5, 80, 158
Third World, 137
  immigration from, 13
timber trade, 29, 42-3
  See also forest industry
Toronto, 8
  in 1867, *illustration*, 35
  as home for immigrants, 13
Toronto Star, cartoon, 111, 140
tourism, Prince Edward Island, 5
trade:
  with Great Britain, 28-9
  with United States, 29, 51
Trans-Canada Highway, 5
treaties, with Indians, 40
treaty rights, and Constitution, 105
Trent (mail ship), 31
Triple-E Senate, 71-2
Trudeau, Pierre, 56, 65, 101, 104, 106, 115, 124, 152-4
  cartoon, 94, 97, 98, 104, 106, 136, 153
  and Charter, 113, 119
  and Communist China, 135, 139
  and Meech Lake, 109
  and Pacific Rim, 138-9
  and Quebec, 93, 95, 99
  and US, 135
  and the West, 154
Trudeau government, 13, 52, 68, 96
Trudeaumania, 154
Turner, John, 106, 156

U
underground economy, 158
Underhill, Frank, 149
unemployment, 54, 59, 149, 158, 160
  insurance, 54, 79
unilingualism, in Quebec, 153

Union Nationale party, 91, 92
union, pursuit of, in Canada, 31-3, 86
United Empire Loyalists, 26
United Farmer governments, 46
United Nations:
  creation of, 130
  General Assembly, 130
  peacekeepers, 133
  Security Council, 130, 131-4
United States:
  independence, 24
  and League of Nations, 128-9
  military alliance with, 135
  ownership in Canada, 51-2
  parliamentary system, 60-1
  and state powers, 76
  thirteen colonies of, 17
Upper Canada. *See* Ontario
uranium, 50
USS Manhattan, cartoon, 140

V
Vancouver, 9
  as home for immigrants, 13
Vancouver Province, 150
Vérendrye, Jean-Baptiste, 21
Vérendrye, Louis-Joseph, 21
Vérendrye, Pierre Gaultier de Varennes, 21
Victoria (BC), 8
Victoria Charter, 102
Victoria, Queen, 34
Vietnam, American policy in, 135-6
Vietnamese boat people, 14
Vimy Ridge, 126-7
Virginia Company, 17
visible minorities, 13, 15
vote for women, 62

W
wage levels, Quebec, 90
wage and price controls, 54
War of 1812, 26-8
war:
  between English and French, 21-2
  Canada's participation in, 89
  of independence, of the thirteen colonies, 25
War Measures Act, 96
Washington, George, 22, 25
Watts, Ronald, 110
welfare, 54-5, 59, 80, 158-60, 159
Wells, Clyde, 107
West:
  immigration to, early 1900s, 43
  negotiation with Indians for, 39-40
  and secession, 154
  securing for Canada, 34-7
  settlement of, 38
wheat, 7-8
and Prairie settlement, 42
"white-collar" workforce, 59
Wilson, Bertha, 123, 124
Winnipeg General Strike (1919), 46
Wolfe, James, 22
women, in labour market, 45, 58-9
worker militancy, 46
workforce, gender differences, 59
World War I, and military service, 126-8
World War II, 48-9, 130
  events prior to, 129

Y
Yugoslavia, 133

Z
Zundel, Ernst, 120-1